THE LITTLE BOOK OF
SECRET
SOCIETIES

THE LITTLE BOOK OF
SECRET
SOCIETIES

50 of the world's most notorious
organizations and how to join them

JOEL LEVY

METRO BOOKS
New York

METRO BOOKS
New York

An Imprint of Sterling Publishing
387 Park Avenue South
New York, NY 10016

METRO BOOKS and the distinctive Metro Books logo are trademarks of
Sterling Publishing Co., Inc.

This 2012 edition published by Metro Books,
by arrangement with Elwin Street Limited

Conceived and produced by
Elwin Street Limited
144 Liverpool Road
London N1 1LA
www.elwinstreet.com

ISBN 978-1-4351-3899-5

For information about custom editions, special sales, and premium and
corporate purchases, please contact Sterling Special Sales at 800-805-5489
or specialsales@sterlingpublishing.com.

Manufactured in China

2 4 6 8 10 9 7 5 3 1

www.sterlingpublishing.com

Contents

Introduction

The world of secret societies is one of shadows and mysteries, myths and misconceptions. Almost nothing you think you know about secret societies is true, yet they are surrounded by so many enigmas that almost anything could be possible. Secret societies may have been the hidden hand in world history since ancient times, accused or suspected of involvement in everything from the birth of Christianity to the French and American Revolutions, the discovery of the New World to 9/11.

Many secret societies protect their privacy by using codewords and symbols – in fact, a special jargon is necessary even to talk about them. Terms used to describe the aims and concerns of secret societies include esoteric, occult, and Hermetic, but what do they mean? Esoteric means "only for the initiated"; in the context of knowledge, it is used to describe teachings or information that can only be understood by those who have been properly prepared or initiated, and are therefore obscure or meaningless to everyone else. Occult means "hidden," and is used in a similar fashion to esoteric. Because it was traditionally applied to describe knowledge of magic and other things considered to be "dark arts," the term "occult" has come to mean magical and sinister. Hermetic refers to a specific body of knowledge, known as the Hermetic corpus because it was supposedly written by the legendary figure Hermes Trismegistus. Hermetic lore includes alchemy, the art and science of spiritual and physical transformation, and other aspects of occult and esoteric knowledge, such as divination (foretelling the future) and magic.

Many secret societies, including the most famous, such as the Freemasons, are concerned with the esoteric, the occult, and the Hermetic. Others are – or are accused of being – concerned with power and political influence. This aspect of politics is sometimes described as parapolitics, in the sense that it is a shadow or parallel world of politics to the one normally experienced. Parapolitical discourse includes conspiracy theories about secret societies.

The term "conspiracy theory" is often used as a blanket term to dismiss or denigrate a point of view; in fact, such theories merit their own lexicon of descriptive jargon, partly because they cover such a wide spectrum of beliefs, plausibility, and rationality. In this book, "conspiracy theory" is used as a fairly neutral term denoting views differing from the conventional or orthodox. More extreme views, which bear little relation to evidence and are predicated on bigotry and distorted versions of history, are denoted as paranoid conspiracy theories.

An unorthodox approach to history, built on speculation and shaky evidence, is described as "alternative history," while the historical narrative that has become standard use for paranoid conspiracy theorists is referred to as the "Plot Theory" of history. First articulated by the mentally-ill fascist Nesta Webster in the early 20th century, the Plot Theory of history views virtually all major historical events as consequences of an overarching global conspiracy, coordinated by secret societies, such as the Freemasons and the Illuminati (see pages 10 and 13). The greatest fear of Plot Theory adherents is the New World Order (NWO), the aim of the Illuminati conspiracy (a one-world government intent on suppressing religion and reducing humanity to slavery). Those who attempt to dismantle the Plot Theory narrative are debunkers or skeptics.

Part One:
Elite Societies

The Freemasons

Probably the oldest secret society still in existence, Freemasons have provided the basis for most other secret societies of modern times.

Place of origin:	Unknown
When:	ca. 17th century
Founder(s):	Unknown
Current status:	Active, worldwide

History

Known as the Masons and the Craft, and sometimes as the Brotherhood, the Freemasons are a deist, free-thinking fraternal order focused on self-improvement, charity, and brotherly love. Claiming to be a society with secrets, rather than a secret society, the Masons employ rituals, passwords, handshakes, and a rich store of symbolism to convey to initiates a message of spiritual exploration and esoteric education. They take their name from their supposed roots in the medieval stonemasons' guilds. The most skilled masons were those who worked on "free" blocks of stone, shaping them using their esoteric knowledge of geometry; similarly, Freemasons are said to work on shaping and perfecting themselves, using the esoteric wisdom they are taught, which includes much sacred geometry. Membership is open to all men of good character (i.e., without a criminal record) who believe in a supreme being.

The earliest uncontested mention of the fraternity is from the diary of Elias Ashmole, who recorded becoming a Mason in 1646. In 1717 the first Grand Lodge was formed in London, and over the next couple of decades Masonry spread rapidly to continental Europe and the Americas. At its peak in the early 20th century there were 8 million Masons and, although it has since declined, the Craft still claims 2 million members today.

The conspiracy theories

According to anti-Masons, the Masons are a corrupt cabal of elite powerbrokers who have controlled much of human history (most notably the American and French Revolutions), acting either as a continuation of or front for other secret societies, such as the Illuminati (see page 13), Rosicrucians (see page 38), or Knights Templar (see page 71). According to their own accounts, they were founded by Templars returning to Scotland from the Crusades (where they had picked up occult knowledge), and they claim to preserve ancient wisdom dating back to the era of Solomon's Temple and before (perhaps even to Atlantis). Their opponents claim that initiates are indoctrinated in anti-Catholic, atheistic principles; preach and plot revolution; and use their networks of influence and cronyism to advance the careers of fellow Masons and enable them to circumvent the law.

Forced to swear terrifying, bloodthirsty oaths during their initiation ceremonies, which reenact ritual murder, they ruthlessly protect their secrets and kill those who break their oaths, claim the conspiracy theorists. A case in point, they say, is the Italian banker Roberto Calvi, linked to a financial scandal involving the Mafia (see page 128) and the Vatican, discovered hanging from Blackfriars Bridge in London in 1982 with bricks in his pockets, emulating Masonic murder myths. According to the wilder fringes of anti-Masonry, the Freemasons may be more than just power-hungry puppetmasters working to implement the New World Order, with supposed evidence that they practice Satanic ritual abuse and worship a demon called Baphomet in blasphemous rites.

Right Masonic symbols on the Human Rights Monument in Paris, France.

The skeptical view

As the biggest secret society in history, the Freemasons have inevitably attracted the most myths and misconceptions. Their own accounts of their origins are probably fanciful; it is unlikely that they developed from the medieval guilds of actual stonemasons, and claimed links to Templars and other groups were invented by 18th- and 19th-century Masons pursuing political or personal agendas. The Masons probably originated as one of dozens of gentlemen's drinking clubs steeped in the 17th-century intellectual vogue for architectural and mathematical esoterica, freethinking, and deism.

Lurid myths and accusations surrounding the Masons have been a consequence of its success and reactionary hostility aroused by its free-thinking precepts. Claims that Masonry guided and inspired the French Revolution originate with the discredited books *Memories Towards a History of Jacobinism* and *Proofs of a Conspiracy,* by Abbé Augustin Barruel and John Robison, respectively. Barruel and Robison claimed that Masonry had been perverted by the Bavarian Illuminati (see page 13) as part of a plot dating back to the demise of the Templars (see page 71). After the Russian Revolution, eccentric British fascist Nesta Webster popularized the Plot Theory of history in her 1922 book *Secret Societies and Subversive Movements*, linking the Masons to an international Jewish-Bolshevik conspiracy to bring about a New World Order. The enduring influence of these pseudohistories can be seen in continued public belief in links between Masons and, for instance, the supposed Masonic symbolism of the streetplan of Washington, D.C.

Global influence: 31/100

Their sheer size and the number of important historical figures among their ranks, from George Washington and Christopher Wren to Brigham Young and Winston Churchill, mean their principles and spirit have probably been influential, especially in Revolutionary America.

How to join

As long as you are male and not a convicted felon, it is remarkably easy – just get in touch with your nearest Lodge.

The Illuminati

An 18th-century offshoot of Freemasonry now identified by paranoid conspiracy theorists as ultimate arch-conspirators behind the New World Order.

Place of origin:	Bavaria
When:	ca. 18th century
Founder(s):	Adam Weishaupt
Current status:	Defunct

History

A number of different organizations have been identified as or have called themselves "Illuminati" – the illuminated or enlightened ones. The most important was the Bavarian Illuminati, a secret society officially instituted in 1776 by Adam Weishaupt, a disputatious young professor of law at the University of Ingolstadt in Bavaria.

Drawing on his knowledge of Masonry and Mystery Religions, and driven by his fervent free-thinking, anti-Catholic, and republican beliefs, Weishaupt set out a charter for an organization with a strict hierarchy and tough initiation rituals. This, he envisaged, would lead mankind to throw off the old shackles of religion, nationhood, and conventional authority and usher in a new dispensation illuminated by the light of reason.

With the help of an influential Mason, Baron von Knigge, Weishaupt successfully recruited hundreds of high-ranking Masons and intellectuals, and within a few years the organization numbered around 2,000 members, including Duke Ferdinand of Brunswick and the writer and polymath, Johann Wolfgang von Goethe. They referred to themselves as "Perfectibilists," or the "pure" and "Illuminated Freemasonry." By 1783, however, the order was riven by internal dissension, while the Bavarian authorities had got wind of its anarchic intentions. Edicts were issued for its suppression, culminating in a decree of 1787 banning membership on pain of death. Weishaupt fled Ingolstadt and the Illuminati appeared to be defunct.

The conspiracy theories

From the start, say the conspiracy theorists, Weishaupt was explicitly bent on world domination, setting out a detailed plan for the overthrow and destruction of established religions, institutions, and nations. Secret charters were revealed – according to one legend when the messenger carrying them was struck by lightning – which proved that once this turmoil had been unleashed, the Illuminati would seize control and rule over all mankind. Conspiracy theorists hold that the order quickly seized control of the Masons – and indeed was probably created by them in the first place as part of an ongoing plan – and survived its apparent suppression. It planned and coordinated the American and French Revolutions, and went on to control most subsequent history.

Today conspiracy theorists claim that the Illuminati control world governments, finance and business, warfare and illness, media and religion. Their members include all major political, corporate, military, and religious leaders, and are often linked to the Zionist-Bolshevik Jewish banking conspiracy. Paranoid conspiracy theorists like David Icke even believe that the Illuminati are Satanists, the Antichrist, flying saucer pilots, aliens, reptilians, child murderers, and cannibals – sometimes all at once. Their aim is to set up a New World Order in which the great mass of humanity is enslaved and/or murdered, so that a tiny elite can rule with absolute power.

Right The all-seeing eye on the dollar bill, a symbol associated with the Illuminati.

The skeptical view

The Illuminati have become a touchstone for every pseudohistorical, delusional, right-wing, fundamentalist, militia nutjob, and the term is used today as shorthand for a variety of anti-Semitic, racist, homophobic, and otherwise distasteful bigotry, but this simply reveals the intellectual poverty of the paranoid conspiracy movement. In reality, the Bavarian Illuminati were a short-lived group of little consequence in practical terms, although their ideas and aims (which, though ambitious, were high-minded and idealistic, rather than despotic and evil) reflected the spirit of the age, so that they may well have exerted important influence on subsequent intellectual and social developments.

Weishaupt himself quickly abandoned his radical precepts on becoming a family man, and by the time of his death in 1830 he was, according to a chronicle kept by his parish church, "reconciled with the Catholic Church, which, as a youthful professor, he had doomed to death and destruction." The legend of the Illuminati was created almost contemporaneously with the organization itself, by the paranoid conspiracy theorists of the era – reactionaries opposed to their progressive and challenging ideals. In a strange reversal, the Illuminati, the same group that was once demonized *by* the establishment, are today vilified *as* the establishment by reactionary forces who feel excluded or alienated from the mainstream.

Global influence: 9/100

There was once a secret society known as the Illuminati, and their ideology was influential, but they bore little resemblance to the monstrous fiction of latterday paranoid conspiracy lore.

How to join

There are modern groups one can join that claim some relationship or descent from the original Illuminati but these claims are fanciful. If you believe the paranoid account, membership is a closed shop, open only to the elite ruling class and/or reptilian space aliens.

The Invisible College

An informal network of scholars in 17th-century England, or perhaps a sinister cabal of technocrats employing their arcane skills to change the course of history?

Place of origin:	England
When:	17th century
Founder(s):	The "Invisibles" – eight occult masters
Current status:	Defunct

History

The Invisible College is the name given to an informal network of scholars and sages in 17th-century England, including scientists Robert Boyle and Robert Hooke, many of whom were involved in setting up the Royal Society, the world's first scientific research institution. The name derives from the Rosicrucian Manifestos (see page 38), which describe a group of eight occult masters known as the "Invisibles" or the "Invisible College."

The conspiracy theories

Fans of the Plot Theory of history (see page 12) argue that the orderly, God-fearing world of medieval Europe was upended by godless, Satanic occultists who called themselves the Rosicrucians, while the Invisible College formed the highest echelon of their hideous army of atheistic technomages. This ultra-elite cell of alchemists, occultists, and astrologers pursued dark research, including early forms of mind control, psychic enhancement, and energy weapons. Hand-picked and initiated by the arch-conspirator code-named Christian Rosenkreutz (probably Sir Francis Bacon or a similarly high-placed scholar of the dark arts), eight scholars steeped in the occult tradition of ages past (handed down by the enemies of civilization since Atlantean times) gathered around his tomb in a circular crypt to practice their dreadful necromancy. They then went forth to foment revolution around Europe, destroy religion, pervert the colonization of the New World, and install a godless technocratic regime to rule mankind with artifacts of horrible power. These Invisibles would pass on their dark knowledge in a chain of initiation that stretched down through the ages, via the Illuminati and the Freemasons to modern incarnations, such as the Bilderbergers and Skull and Bones, counting dangerous thinkers from Isaac Newton to Albert Einstein among their elite ranks.

The skeptical view

The English "College" was inspired by the writings of statesman and philosopher of science Sir Francis Bacon (1561–1626) , who had probably corresponded with the authors of the Rosicrucian Manifestos. In his work he spoke of a society of natural philosophers (the term "scientist" did not yet exist) working to master the secrets of nature and transform society. But to make the leap to Bacon as the Rosicrucian grandmaster recruiting an elite, super-secret cadre of natural philosophers is pure fiction. Bacon was not a Rosicrucian because no one was (the Rosicrucians did not exist as a real society – see page 38), and Bacon's philosophy was explicitly opposed to secrecy. The Invisible College was never a real secret society, only a loose coalition of scholars retrospectively labeled. Like most of the leading intellects of the day, including many clerics, these philosophers were fascinated by the ancient wisdom apparently offered by alchemy and what they termed "natural magic" (essentially a protoscientific system of knowledge), but they were also deeply religious and often strong nationalists, with little sympathy for radical or revolutionary sentiments.

Global influence: 45/100

The influence of this group of scholars is incalculable in terms of their role in fomenting the Scientific Revolution. However, in conspiracy terms they had little or no influence.

How to join

Travel back in time to the late 17th century; learn Greek, Hebrew, and Latin; study alchemy, cabala, astrology, Biblical history, and mathematics for at least 30 years; then write to Robert Boyle, care of the Royal Society, London.

Skull and Bones

A Yale University
undergraduate secret society
with a history of famous
alumni, accused of being a
nursery for the elite
controllers of the New World

Place of origin:	USA
When:	1832
Founder(s):	William H. Russell
Current status:	Active, Yale

Order, training them to govern global capitalism,
the secret state, and the drug trade.

History

Yale University is one of America's oldest and the world's most prestigious
academic institutions, boasting a long history of secret societies that select elite
candidates for esoteric rituals and heavy drinking. The most infamous of these
societies was founded in 1832 by William H. Russell after a visit to Germany
where he probably came across similar societies thriving in German colleges.
Initially named the Eulogian Club, the society was renamed in 1833 after taking
a pirate flag as its emblem.

Every year the Skull and Bones taps 15 new seniors to become members
(exclusively men until 1991). Meetings and quasi-Masonic ceremonies are held
at the Society's headquarters, known as the tomb, reportedly amid theatrically
Gothic trappings. Past alumni, or Bonesmen, have included three Presidents
(William Howard Taft, George H. Bush, and George W. Bush), numerous
Cabinet members and senators, and many captains of industry.

The conspiracy theories

A circle of elite families have controlled America since its founding, say
conspiracy paranoiacs, maintaining a façade of democracy while growing fat
off the proceeds of the arms and drugs trade – and Skull and Bones is where
these conspirators against the American people are recruited and trained. It
is particularly noted by opponents for its supposedly strong links to the

Above Illustration of the Skull and Bones society building at Yale University.

intelligence community and illicit establishment involvement in protecting and promoting drug trafficking, which dates back to the 19th-century opium trade. The corrupt networks of influence established at Skull and Bones permeate the top echelons of American power, conspiracy theorists hold, claiming this was graphically demonstrated by the 2004 U.S. presidential election, in which the American people were presented with a "choice" between George W. Bush and John Kerry, both Bonesmen. More specifically, Skull and Bones has been accused of perpetuating a cult of death through its morbid rituals and symbolism, signposting its role as the nursery for the Illuminati elite bloodlines behind the New World Order.

The skeptical view

Dark fantasies about the reach and power of Skull and Bones fly in the face of the evidence – it is not even the most exclusive or secret society at Yale, let alone in America, argue the skeptics. Little more than a souped-up frat house, Skull and Bones has few secrets that have not been exposed, and a surprisingly progressive recruitment policy at odds with ludicrous accusations concerning elite bloodlines. While important figures in American power politics have been and continue to be Bonesmen, this is as much an expression of the prestige of Yale. Most of the nation's elite, after all, are not Bonesmen.

Having said which, self-selecting clubs that inevitably lead to networks of influence are inherently anti-democratic. The soiled reputation and record of the American military-intelligence complex means there are questions to be answered about the role of Bonesmen in the secret state, but this does not necessarily implicate Skull and Bones itself.

Global influence: 19/100

Bonesmen like George W. Bush, his father, George H. Bush, and his grandfather, Prescott Bush, all involved in politics, the CIA, and the corporate arm of the military-industrial complex, demonstrate the enduring influence of the society's alumni, but it is not clear that Skull and Bones itself is more than a frat house.

How to join

Gain admittance to Yale, develop an impressive record of public service and lofty political ambitions, cultivate the right people, and cross your fingers. Alternatively, sell your soul to join an Illuminati bloodline, possibly by modifying your genome with reptilian alien DNA.

Bilderberg

Every year the American and European elite meets at a top hotel for secret discussions, yet until recently the media kept strangely silent.

Place of origin:	The Netherlands
When:	1954
Founder(s):	Multiple (see below)
Current status:	Defunct

History

The Bilderberg meetings are named after the Dutch hotel where the first of these informal annual gatherings took place in 1954. The meeting was the brainchild of Prince Bernhard of the Netherlands, Polish diplomat Joseph Retinger, international banker David Rockefeller, and former British Foreign Minister Denis Healey. Setting a template that has been followed ever since, they drew up a guest list of the important and up-and-coming figures from the worlds of politics, business, and the media and invited them to a swanky hotel. Almost 60 years on, the Bilderbergers still meet, but until recently coverage of their activities has been confined to the conspiracy community and fringe activists.

The conspiracy theories

For conspiracy paranoiacs, Bilderberg is a breathtakingly brazen annual gathering of the New World Order elite, where the ruling agenda for the next year is cooked up. They allege that the founders include a Dutch prince whose wartime role and links to the Nazis have been questioned; a Polish diplomat suspected to have been in the pay of the CIA and MI6; and a scion of the international banking family accused of squatting at the heart of the dark web of the Illuminati-Zionist-Bolshevik conspiracy, pulling the strings of the New World Order.

The power of Bilderberg is supposedly confirmed by a brief glance at the roster of attendees, which has included almost every major power-broker in postwar transatlantic history, and, in particular, presidents and prime ministers before they came to power. Candidates deemed to show clear promise are invited to Bilderberg to be groomed for their roles, before being anointed and sent back to participate in their sham democracies, say its critics. Most likely both "choices" in any given election are Bilderbergers. In addition, the group sets military and financial policy for the year ahead. For instance, Bilderberg is accused by some of having given the go-ahead for the NATO action against Serbia in the 1990s. For most of its history Bilderberg was restricted to American and European attendees, thus excluding most of the global population from representation.

Such a clear violation of democratic principles has only been possible because of the compliance of the mainstream media, say the conspiracy theorists. Major media figures are among the attendees, and so must be compliant with the media blackout, they reason. Supposedly, those attempting to report on and/or investigate the conference are subject to surveillance and harassment by heavies in black suits, driving unmarked black vehicles, in addition to local security forces duped into cooperation.

The skeptical view

The Bilderberg meetings are private, not secret, and this privacy is essential to allow open and wide-ranging discussion, say the organization's defenders. The nature of the guest list necessitates heavy security, and any mistreatment of

would-be interlopers can be put down to unintentional heavy-handedness and the challenge of dealing with aggressive intruders.

Bilderberg has always been fairly open about its goals – to facilitate open discourse between important decision-makers and opinion-makers, with the aim of strengthening the liberal, democratic, free-market political philosophy of the free world. The meetings were started during the Cold War, with anticommunism as

Left Prince Bernhard, one of the founders of the Bilderberg meetings.

the driving force; but even with the fall of the Iron Curtain, the free-market agenda is still relevant and modern liberal democracies face a range of challenges that merit free and frank debate among those tasked with overcoming them. The Bilderberg steering committee publishes a guest list and a schedule of discussion topics, and has recently become even more open with a website established at Bilderbergmeetings.org.

Accusations that Bilderberg chooses future leaders miss the point. The steering committee is good at spotting the most promising up-and-coming talent, and the identities of the next generation of political leaders is often obvious. More to the point, conspiracy theorists are selective in their choice of evidence, ignoring the list of invitees who have not gone on to hold high office. Accusations leveled at the group's founders and subsequent attendees are for the most part distasteful fantasies linked to fringe reactionary and anti-Semitic agendas.

Global influence: 50/100

Bilderberg tries to defend itself by claiming to be open about issues such as guest lists and discussion topics, but these claims are misleading. The published guest list is always incomplete, and the information given is bland and meaningless (for example, the 2011 conference included a discussion on "Social Networks: Connectivity and Security Issues"). But the real problem is that even if Bilderberg is as well-intentioned as it claims, it is a powerful challenge to democratic principles. Billionaires and corporate CEOs get to network with/lobby policy-makers, with no oversight or accountability. Elected officials refuse to inform their electorates what was discussed, but we know that Bilderberg relentlessly pushes an agenda of free-market capitalism and globalization. This agenda is riddled with problems, as recent events have clearly demonstrated, yet electorates are allowed no input or insight into the process. While conspiracy theories linking Bilderberg to Illuminati fantasies may be nonsense, the world's premier talking shop is patently undemocratic.

How to join

Make a billion dollars, get elected to high office, or make friends with a member of the steering committee.

Bohemian Grove

The ancient redwoods of
northern California host an
annual event steeped in
theatrical rituals – but is
it all merely playacting?

Place of origin:	USA
When:	1872
Founder(s):	Multiple
Current status:	Active, USA

History

Bohemian Grove is an area of forest not far from San Francisco, where more than 2,000 of America's male elite – almost entirely white, Christian, and elderly – gather every summer in luxurious cabin and camp accommodation. The camp was started in 1872 by the Bohemian Club, a society for San Francisco journalists, but it has since become an event for the Republican elite, who stay in "campsites" equipped with bars and hot tubs, drink heavily, walk in the woods, attend lectures and seminars, and enjoy the entertainment.

Controversy centers on the quasi-Masonic ritual element of the camp, which includes a ceremony known as the Cremation of Care. As the assembled Grovers watch from the shores of a small lake, men dressed in red robes gravely mimic the sacrifice of a small effigy known as "Dull Care," which is then placed in a small boat adorned with a skull and set alight.

The conspiracy theories

At best, say the conspiracy theorists, Bohemian Grove is another example of an exclusive club where a tiny self-selecting elite circumvent democratic process and public oversight by meeting in secret. The guest list includes (or has included) almost every major figure from right-wing politics, including Dick Cheney, Karl Rove, Donald Rumsfeld, Henry Kissinger, both George Bushes, David and Nelson Rockefeller, Ronald Reagan, and Gerald Ford. With a hefty $25,000 entry fee and a 15-year waiting list, the Bohemian Club is beyond the reach of ordinary Americans, even if they were allowed to join.

Charges of simple elitism and antidemocratic powertrading pale by comparison with some of the accusations leveled against Grovers. According to one school of thought, the Cremation of Care is more than merely playacting – it is a genuine human sacrifice. "Dull Care" is a real child, sacrificed to a Satanic god. The Cremation of Care is a symbolic sacrifice of Jesus, and is accompanied by the ritual abuse and murder of hundreds of other children abducted from across America, as the degenerate Grovers – in actuality, members of the vile Illuminati-bloodline dynasties – engage in sordid, orgiastic rites.

The skeptical view

The deranged fantasies of mass human sacrifice have no basis in fact. Skeptics contend that Bohemian Grove is an eccentric but harmless summer camp for old white guys, where the main activities are drinking and urinating against trees. A typical program of events contains musical acts, comedy skits, drag acts, and lectures on forestry and energy security. The guest list might have included Dick Cheney and Henry Kissinger, but it has also featured Mark Twain, Clint Eastwood, and at least two former members of the Grateful Dead.

The Cremation of Care is a much misunderstood piece of theater, representing the symbolic destruction of the cares and stresses of the world at the start of the summer camp, and was typical of 19th-century Masonic-influenced theater. Even the charge that corporate interests have unfair access to policy-makers is wide of the mark. The Bohemian Club's motto is, "Weaving spiders come not here" – i.e., no talking business or networking. In truth, the most sinister accusation that can be leveled at the Club is that it has an irresponsible forestry policy and is trying to cut down too many ecologically valuable trees.

Global influence: 23/100

Bohemian Grove is probably not an epic setting for Satanic depravity, but as with the Bilderberg meetings, guarded conclaves where the ruling elite meet without oversight or public scrutiny are antidemocratic by nature.

How to join

Apart from paying $25,000 to get on the waiting list (and $5,000 a year once you're a member), you will need the right connections. Attend an elite prep school, graduate to an Ivy League university, become chief executive of a major arms manufacturer, and make sure to donate a lot of money to Republican Party causes.

MJ-12

MJ-12, short for Majestic-12, is supposedly a super-secret, supra-governmental committee set up to oversee relations between humanity and alien invaders intent on colonizing the Earth.

Place of origin:	USA
When:	1947
Founder(s):	President Truman
Current status:	Fictional hoax

History

Documents that came to light in 1987, supposedly supplied by anonymous government "insiders" to conspiracy and ufology researchers, William Moore and Stanton Friedman, appeared to be classified military briefings revealing the existence of a mysterious and shadowy organization known as MJ-12. This 12-man committee, which included leading figures from the military, scientific, and intelligence communities, including Vannevar Bush and James Forrestal, was code-named Majic-12, itself short for Majestic-12. It soon became instrumental in a conspiracy of mind-blowing proportions that sounds like the plot of a movie or TV series, linking the Roswell incident, alien abductions, cattle mutilations, secret government black-ops, and the New World Order.

The conspiracy theories

The MJ-12 documents apparently revealed that after the 1947 Roswell incident, involving a crashed alien flying saucer and the retrieval of its occupants, President Truman set up the eponymous committee to keep a lid on the UFO issue. In 1952, President Dwight D. Eisenhower, allegedly directed it to continue its work in the light of subsequent saucer crash incidents.

However, this was just the jumping-off point for an increasingly fantastic tale spun by the conspiracy/ufology community, in which a series of close encounters culminated in a meeting in 1954 at Holloman Air Force Base where

Above Brig. General Ramey and Col. Dubose identify metallic fragments found near Roswell as pieces of a weather balloon, the basis of the supposed crash of an alien spacecraft, 1947.

MJ-12 made a deal with a race of aliens known as the Greys. In return for alien technology to maintain their grip on power, MJ-12 would assist the Greys in their attempts to use terrestrial genetic material to breed an alien-human hybrid race that would take over the world. The committee formed a black-ops unit, equipped with silent black helicopters, to aid the aliens in their cattle-mutilation and human-abduction experiments, conducted from bases, such as the legendary Area 51.

MJ-12, conspiracy theorists hold, mutated into a pan-governmental secret state, with its own security services, funded through arms and drugs trafficking, controlling postwar history to cement its grip on power and prepare the way for the New World Order. MJ-12 used reverse-engineered alien technology to construct its own military hardware, and employed programs like MK-ULTRA (see page 29) to develop mind-control technologies and orchestrate Manchurian Candidate scenarios. Anyone who got in the way of MJ-12's plans was assassinated – hence the death of President John F. Kennedy, according to some. For Christian fundamentalist conspiracy theorists, MJ-12 is helping to prepare the way for the Apocalypse.

The skeptical view

The MJ-12 documents have been proven to be forgeries and hoaxes (given away by the anachronistic typeface and dating system, for instance). More interesting is the question of how they came into the hands of Moore and Friedman. They may have been involved in the hoax, but it has also since emerged that the USAF did orchestrate a disinformation campaign to feed bogus "insider" material to ufologists, possibly to help cover up genuine secret research projects.

Global influence: 3/100

MJ-12 never existed, but as a fictional entity it has influenced both UFO and conspiracy research and infiltrated popular culture, as evidenced by the appearance of similar organizations in the *X-Files* and the movie *Independence Day*.

How to join

Only those at the pinnacle of the global conspiracy with alien colonists are eligible, and even then you would need to bump off one of the existing members to free up a spot.

MK-ULTRA

A CIA-sponsored covert research program into mind control, particularly the use of psychedelic drugs and brainwashing, supposedly halted in the 1960s.

Place of origin:	USA
When:	1953–1961
Founder(s):	Unknown
Current status:	Defunct

History

In one of the darkest chapters of the history of the American security establishment, the CIA oversaw an extensive program of research into mind-control techniques that included widespread dosing of unsuspecting subjects with psychedelic drugs. The program, known as MK-ULTRA, began in 1953 but its roots were in existing CIA and Navy programs called Artichoke and Chatter.

All of these programs were inspired by fear over alleged communist advances in the field – it was believed that the Soviet Union had developed "truth drugs," while footage of American troops captured during the Korean War and apparently brainwashed into parroting communist propaganda terrified the public and military alike (inspiring the book and movie *The Manchurian Candidate*). MK-ULTRA was intended to give the US the ability to both resist and counteract these communist threats, and between 1953 and 1961 the program, under the supervision of Dr. Sidney Gottlieb, used hypnotism, drugs, behavioral modification, radiation, manipulation of sleep patterns, enhanced interrogation, and even electroshock therapy to pursue these ends.

The most sensational programs were those involving the use of LSD, which culminated in Operation Midnight Climax, in which the CIA rented apartments, employed prostitutes to bring back unwitting subjects, dosed them with LSD, and observed the effects. Such operations resulted in at least one death, that of CIA officer Frank Olsen, who fell from an 11th-story window, apparently committing suicide after having unknowingly taken LSD. The program was officially halted in 1961 after it became clear the technologies did not work, and although many of the files on the project were illegally destroyed by the CIA director Richard Helms (who had personally overseen MK-ULTRA) in 1972, hearings in Congress uncovered much of the truth.

The conspiracy theories

Claims that MK-ULTRA was shut down in 1961 are dismissed as a flimsy cover by conspiracy theorists. They claim that the project continued, and was responsible for creating the youth counterculture of the 1960s as a form of mass mind control, subverting youthful rebellion into harmless, mind-addling drug abuse. Psychedelic apostle Timothy Leary was, they say, actually working for the CIA. In fact, paranoiacs claim that military personnel were never the primary target of MK-ULTRA operations – the goal was always to develop mass mind-control technology to manipulate the American people. Mind-control techniques created Manchurian Candidates to murder JFK, RFK, Martin Luther King, and others. Today, MK-ULTRA is accused of continuing to serve the Illuminati NWO as Project Monarch, using advanced techniques such as Extremely Low Frequency radio waves to transmit orders to legions of brainwashed stooges, who are frequently misdiagnosed as schizophrenics, paranoiacs, and alien abductees.

The skeptical view

MK-ULTRA was a terrible abuse, but its failure demonstrates the fictional basis for continuing claims of mind-control conspiracy. Even today neuroscience cannot explain, let alone control, most mental processes.

Global influence: 29/100

Many mysteries remain about the extent and effect of MK-ULTRA's activities and its role in the secret history of the Cold War. Beyond this, the covert operation has undoubtedly had considerable cultural and social influence, with enduring consequences.

How to join

Join the army, get assigned to intelligence, gain degrees in neurobiology and toxicology, and display a willingness to test radical theories on human subjects – you may be recruited to Project Monarch.

The John Birch Society

Right-wing society formed in the late 1950s to oppose what its founders believed was a widespread communist conspiracy.

Place of origin:	USA
When:	1958
Founder(s):	Robert Welch
Current status:	Active, USA

History

Founded in 1958 by candy-manufacturing businessman Robert Welch, the John Birch Society took its name from Captain John Birch, an American missionary and intelligence officer killed by Chinese Communists at the end of the Second World War. Welch held extreme right-wing views and believed that a vast communist conspiracy threatened the world, and more specifically had poisoned the American body politic, to the point where even the Republican Party was far too moderate. In the 1960s, the fanatical anticommunism of Welch and his followers was enormously influential.

Although the JBS courted publicity, it kept its membership secret and worked to influence policy-makers and infiltrate grassroots politics. The high point of JBS influence came in 1964, when it was instrumental in shifting the Republican Party to the right, culminating in the selection of Barry Goldwater as the 1964 presidential candidate. In the wake of his defeat, Welch's conspiracy theories grew more extreme and the JBS became a fringe organization with dwindling membership, although opposition to Obama and an increase in extreme parapolitical beliefs has led to a recent upsurge.

The conspiracy theories

The JBS has been widely accused of involvement in precisely the Illuminati conspiracies it sought to denounce. According to some paranoid conspiracy theorists, the JBS is a classic "double bubble" stratagem, in which a false dichotomy is created (in this case between the extreme right-wing JBS and their extreme left-wing opponents) to conceal from the populace a greater truth. In this reading, the JBS are actually an Illuminati front created to spread disinformation and coopt people into becoming Illuminati dupes.

The skeptical view

Skeptics argue that JBS members are not merely pretending to be foaming-at-the-mouth right-wing fanatics with absurd delusions of Communist-Illuminati conspiracy and a bizarre revisionist view of history – they really are. The skeptical view of the JBS, however, begins to shade into conspiracy territory when it comes to its influence on contemporary political and parapolitical discourse, with claims that the same corporate-capitalist forces that were behind the creation and promotion of the JBS are today driving the Tea Party movement, in many senses its direct descendant. The Tea Party movement seems to have taken both its parapolitical beliefs and its political mechanisms (such as grassroots political action) from the same playbook as the JBS, and this is probably more than a coincidence.

Global influence: 26/100

The JBS is now a fringe organization and paranoid conspiracy claims about its role strangle themselves with their own double-bluffing complexity. In the past,

however, the JBS has been a major player in American politics, with an enduring and increasingly potent legacy in contemporary political discourse.

How to join

The website of the John Birch Society invites applications to join or form chapters.

Left Robert Welch, November 24, 1961.

The Elders of Zion

Nonexistent cabal of Jews whose alleged plans for world domination were set out in their Protocols - in reality, a crude hoax cooked up by anti-Semitic propagandists.

Place of origin:	Russia
When:	1905
Founder(s):	Unknown
Current status:	Fictional hoax

History

The Protocols of the Elders of Zion is claimed to be the secret minutes of meetings of the eponymous Elders, which set out their cunning plans for world domination. The *Protocols* first appeared in Russia in 1905 and were recycled in 1920 by the *Dearborn Independent*, a newspaper belonging to American industrialist Henry Ford. Articles from the *Independent* were collected as a book, *The International Jew: The World's Foremost Problem*, which was an influence on Adolf Hitler, who referenced the *Protocols* in his own work. Despite repeatedly being debunked, the *Protocols* are still referenced as genuine documents by some contemporary conspiracy paranoiacs, especially those who are openly or cryptically anti-Semitic.

The conspiracy theories

The *Protocols* contain risibly grandiose and fiendish instructions for Illuminati-style global conspirators. For instance, Article 2 of Protocol 2 records the Elders gloating that, "The administrators ... from among the public ... will easily become pawns in our game, specially bred from childhood to rule the affairs of the whole world." They read more like satire than reality (this is because they are: see page 35). But adherents of the Plot Theory of history claim that the Elders are none other than the Illuminati, or a branch thereof, and representative of the centuries-long campaign by the global Jewish conspiracy to subvert Christiandom and subjugate the Earth. Identification of shape-shifting reptilian aliens as the true Illuminati villains is usually a thinlyveiled code for "Jews," and the *Protocols* are often adduced to bolster such fantasies.

The skeptical view

The *Protocols* are a notorious forgery and hoax, which have been repeatedly unmasked and debunked. They reside at the toxic intersection of the Plot Theory of history, originated by the anti-Masonic writings of Robison and Barruel (see page 12), and the millennia-long history of anti-Semitic propaganda, such as the notorious Blood Libel. The Blood Libel is the claim that Jews engage in human sacrifice, usually the murder of Christian children, for ritual purposes (for example, blood is supposedly used in the production of unleavened bread). Such claims date back to before the Christian era, and sparked off numerous pogroms (anti-Semitic riots) in medieval and modern times. Blood Libel is a common element of paranoid conspiracy claims about human sacrifices in the context of, for example, Bohemian Grove (see page 24) or the Knights Templar (see page 71). It was believed that this ritual sacrifice was organized by an international conspiracy of Jews, providing a template for anti-Semitism and anti-Illuminati Plot Theories to come together in the 19th century.

These ideas reached their fruition in late 19th-century Russia, where agents in the service of the Czar were charged with producing anti-Semitic propaganda.

Above An 18th-century painting of the infamous anti-semitic myth Blood Libel.

Working with the secret police, an extreme anti-Semite named Mathieu Golovinski put together the *Protocols*, which were adduced as evidence to justify state repression of Russian Jews when they appeared in 1905. *The Times* of London exposed Golovinski's work as crude plagiarism in a series of articles in 1920, identifying them as straightforward copies of Maurice Joly's 1864 tract, *Dialogue In Hell Between Machiavelli and Montesquieu*, written as a satire on the grandiose plans of the French Emperor, Napoleon III. Golovinski simply replaced "Napoleon" with "Jews." Joly's *Dialogue* in turn was lifted from an earlier work slandering the Jesuits.

Despite the exposé in *The Times*, Ford's *Dearborn Independent* recycled the Protocols and they became firmly established in the English-speaking conspiracy world. They remain one of the most disturbing examples of the way in which conspiracy theories can be used to demonize groups or ethnicities, with genuine and tragic consequences over the years. Much of the wilder speculation of the paranoid conspiracy world, from right-wing claims that the American Civil Liberties Union is an agent of Illuminati repression to left-wing belief in the malign power of "international bankers," should be seen in the context of Protocol-style conspiracy accusations.

Global influence: 0/100

The Elders of Zion are entirely fictional. The fake document known as the *Protocols* has been influential, however, in propagating the anti-Semitic themes that have become entrenched in paranoid conspiracy lore and Plot Theory fantasies. The *Protocols* are still cited as evidence today, just as they were throughout the 20th century.

How to join

According to the *Protocols*, everyone from the Masons to the Illuminati are simply fronts for the Elders of Zion, so joining any of these conspiracies entails membership of the wider plot. For anti-Semitic conspiracy paranoiacs, anyone Jewish is automatically suspected of potential involvement.

Part Two:

Mystical and Occult Societies

The Rosicrucians

Founded by legendary figure Christian Rosenkreutz, the Rosicrucians were supposedly an elite cadre of magician-scholars working to transform Early Modern Europe.

Place of origin:	Unknown
When:	ca. 1407
Founder(s):	Christian Rosenkreutz
Current status:	Fictional

History

In the early 17th century, European intellectuals were abuzz with excitement over the publication of three documents purporting to reveal the existence of a secret society known as the Brotherhood of the Rosy Cross, or Rosicrucians. Between 1614 and 1616, German printers issued copies of three works – *Report of the Rosicrucians, Confession of the Brotherhood,* and *The Chymical Wedding of Christian Rosenkreutz* – collectively known as the Rosicrucian Manifestos. They recounted the exploits of a medieval nobleman who went by the pseudonym Christian Rosenkreutz, born in Germany in 1380. Rosenkreutz was said to have traveled in the Orient and studied the occult, before returning to Germany and founding a college to teach a select band of eight initiates (known as the Invisible College – see page 16) his unique brand of religious, scientific, medical, and occult wisdom. After his death at the age of 104, Rosenkreutz was buried in an octagonal vault and his disciples charged with continuing his work in secret until it was time to reveal themselves and effect a total revolution in human affairs. According to the Manifestos, the rediscovery of Rosenkreutz's tomb in 1604 was the trigger for this revelation.

The Manifestos comprise a potent stew of symbolism and allegory (the rose and the cross, for instance, are richly symbolic devices relating to feminine and masculine virtues, the elements, religion, and many other areas). The secrets they reveal seem to relate to alchemy; the recovery of ancient wisdom; theosophy; and the need for spiritual, moral, philosophical, and political revolution.

Despite official condemnation, some of Europe's leading scholars wrote openly in support of the Rosicrucians. The English physician and alchemist

Robert Fludd and the German diplomat, physician, and alchemist Michael Maier both penned tracts praising the newly revealed fraternity. Possibly the first person to go on record as becoming a Rosicrucian was the English antiquarian and diarist Elias Ashmole, who noted that in 1646 he and others, including the astrologer William Lilly, founded a Rosicrucian lodge in London.

The conspiracy theories

Conspiracy theorists take the Manifestos at face value, believing that they reveal the existence and workings of a super-secret society explicitly dedicated to global revolution. Of particular interest is the real identity of Christian Rosenkreutz and his leading disciples, the Invisibles. The Manifestos have strong parallels with the work of the mystic Jakob Boehme, founder of theosophy; astrologer, magician and scholar Dr. John Dee; and statesman and philosopher of science Sir Francis Bacon – all these men have been suggested as the real Rosenkreutz, along with figures from Leonardo da Vinci to William Shakespeare. Candidates for the Invisibles include every major mystic, philosopher, artist, and occultist of the last 400 years, from Isaac Newton to Picasso. The Rosicrucians are said to have founded the Freemasons and fomented every major revolution, including the American, French, and Russian Revolutions.

The skeptical view

The paper trail of the Manifestos leads nowhere. Looking for the "true" identity of Christian Rosenkreutz and the Invisibles is fruitless, because

Symbolisme de la Rose-Croix.

Right Symbolic representation of the Rosy Cross with astrological and alchemical additions.

the Rosicrucians never existed. The third and last of the Manifestos, the *Chymical Wedding,* is generally attributed to German theologian Johann Valentin Andreae, and the other two are believed to have been penned by Andreae and the Tübingen circle (a group of scholars centered on Tübingen University, Andreae among them). These men concocted the Manifestos as a sort of literary parlor game, possibly with input or feedback from Boehme, Bacon, Fludd, Maier, and others – all of whom were more or less in on the joke. Their fictional creation was so successful it prompted some Freemasons, such as Ashmole and Lilly, to ape their name and some of their modish concerns. Such copycats are more properly termed "pseudo-Rosicrucians," a category that took on a life of its own, spawning societies such as the Order of the Golden and Rosy Cross (see page 41)and the *Societas Rosicruciana* (see page 46). Of more interest than the identity of the Rosicrucian hoaxers is the question of why the Manifestos were published at all. According to one theory, the Rosicrucian agenda was a strongly Protestant one and the Manifestos were intended to rally support for the Protestant prince of the Rhine Palatinate, Frederick V, in his battle with the Catholic Hapsburgs for the throne of Bohemia.

Global influence: 27/100

Although the Rosicrucians were almost certainly a literary creation, they were remarkably influential for fictional characters. Rosicrucian ideas percolated through intellectual culture and helped inspire, for instance, the founding of the Royal Society in London (see The Invisible College, page 16).

How to join

Locate the hidden tomb of Christian Rosenkreutz (identifiable by its octagonal crypt) somewhere in Germany. Once there, make contact with one of the Invisibles and impress him with your encyclopaedic knowledge of natural philosophy, theosophy, and the occult.

Order of the Golden and Rosy Cross

German Masonic order claiming Rosicrucian heritage, which introduced alchemy and the occult to Freemasonry and briefly became the power behind the Prussian throne in the late 18th century.

Place of origin:	Germany
When:	1750s–1790s
Founder(s):	Herman Fichtuld
Current status:	Defunct

History

In 1710, under the pseudonym Sincerus Renatus, Sigmund Richter published what purported to be the laws of the Brotherhood of the Golden and Rosy Cross. Around 40 years later, German alchemist Herman Fichtuld founded a new Masonic order based on the work of Renatus, calling it the *Orden des Gold und Rosenkreuz*, or Order of the Golden and Rosy Cross (OGRC). Only Master Masons (the third and highest degree of basic Masonry) could join, starting at the degree of Junior. By following a program of alchemical and occult research, including practical experiments, they could progress through eight further degrees: Theoreticus, Practicus, Philosophus, Adeptus Minor, Adeptus Major, Adeptus Exemptus, Magister, and Magus.

The OGRC claimed to have been founded in the first days of the Christian era by Ormus, an Egyptian magician who had converted to the new religion and combined his ancient Egyptian lore with the mystical philosophy of Jesus and the Essenes (a Gnostic Jewish sect from around the time of Jesus).

The OGRC was popular with aristocratic German Masons, including the crown prince of Prussia, Frederich Wilhelm II. He joined in 1781; five years later his father died and he came to the Prussian throne, bringing the OGRC to a position of prominence and influence. This influence lasted only as long as his rule; on his death in 1797 the society fell from grace, apparently breaking up shortly afterward during the chaos of the Napoleonic Wars.

The conspiracy theories

Both the wider alternative history/conspiracy theory community and the OGRC's own Legend of Perpetuation view the OGRC as part of the founding myth of the Freemasons. According to this view, Ormus' ancient Order of the Rose Cross had eventually been brought to Europe by Templars returning from the Crusades, and was bound up with the supposed genesis of Freemasonry. Templars in Scotland were said to have created Freemasonry as a vehicle for their Rosicrucian wisdom, a sort of shop window for recruiting and preparing suitable candidates for the higher-order secrets of the OGRC. Through their control over Frederich Wilhelm, the OGRC were able to set up lasting Rosicrucian institutions; more specifically, the OGRC was linked in a direct line of initiation to subsequent Rosicrucian societies such as *Societas Rosicruciana* (see page 46) and the Hermetic Order of the Golden Dawn (see page 48).

The skeptical view

The OGRC was simply a pseudo-Rosicrucian offshoot of Freemasonry, with no more antique lineage than the Masons themselves (i.e., none). It was cobbled together to satisfy the contemporary vogue in Germany for esoterica with a reactionary flavor, stealing most of its structure from Richter's book of laws. The OGRC's only link with later pseudo-Rosicrucian societies was through a similar process, and its brief flirtation with genuine political influence came to an abrupt end, with no lasting consequences.

Global influence: 22/100

As one of the few secret societies genuinely to wield some political and cultural power, albeit briefly, the OGRC can claim to have actually influenced history. In terms of later esoteric societies, its structure and pursuits were very influential.

How to join

No longer exists, but if it did you would need to become a Master Mason, gain an aristocratic title in Germany, study alchemy and the occult, and hope to be approached.

The Theosophical Society

The Theosophical Society continues to offer occult wisdom concerning Atlantis, psychic powers, and the secret history of the last million years.

Place of origin:	USA
When:	1875
Founder(s):	Helena Blavatsky
Current status:	Active, worldwide

History

Though not strictly secret, the Theosophical Society has been hugely influential on the evolution of subsequent occult and esoteric societies, with which it shares many features and beliefs. The Society was created in New York in 1875 by Russian émigré Helena Petrovna Blavatsky, better known as Madame Blavatsky, a self-proclaimed psychic and seer with a remarkable life story. Blavatsky was born into a Russian aristocratic family and introduced to esoteric mysteries by her great-grandfather, a Rosicrucian Freemason. She claimed to have studied magic and mysticism in Istanbul and Cairo, and have possessed psychic powers since childhood. Most contentiously, Blavatsky said that she had visited Tibet and studied with immortal super-powered sages known as Ascended Masters, who had instructed her in the hidden history of human evolution – an amazing story of millions of years of racial warfare, lost civilizations, and psychic powers.

In the 1870s Blavatsky was in Cairo, earning money by exhibiting her psychic gifts and working as a spiritualist medium. Chased out of Egypt after allegations of fraud, which were to dog her throughout her life, she moved to America. In New York she gained her most important follower, lawyer and journalist Henry Steel Olcott. Together they founded the Theosophical Society to promulgate Blavatsky's version of theosophy, apparently at the bidding of her Ascended Masters, who helpfully penned a series of letters setting out their wisdom. The Theosophical Society attempted to synthesize a range of Oriental religions, philosophies, and mysteries with a scientific outlook. Perhaps its most controversial teachings were Blavatsky's revelations about Root Races – races

Above Drawing from a contemporary American newspaper, depicting Elenea Petrovna Blavatsky (left) at a seance of dubious authenticity in 1873. Accusations of fraud dogged her career.

from the early stages of human evolution, who had battled each other, with evil, dark-skinned races attempting to defeat noble, light-skinned ones.

The Society grew rapidly, thanks to its heady blend of spiritualism, exotic Eastern religion, and modish scientific trappings, and the popularity of Blavatsky's books. Its headquarters were moved to India in 1882, and although it suffered a blow when investigators from the Society for Psychical Research declared Blavatsky a fraud in 1885, the Theosophical Society survived and is still going strong today, with branches around the world.

The conspiracy theories

Blavatsky's Theosophy is the original source of many elements of the conspiracy theory universe (for example, the secret cabal of occult masters guiding human history from a base in the Himalayas, the existence of Atlantis, and the epic pre-historic narrative pitting the noble defenders of humanity against the degenerate subhuman Illuminati, in an unending race war). Paranoid conspiracy theorists of a fundamentalist bent see Theosophy as another brand of Satanic New Age brainwashing and/or part of a larger Illuminati conspiracy to twist the truth about human history.

The skeptical view

Madame Blavatsky was a charlatan and hoaxer; her Ascended Masters were a transparent invention, and she simply mashed together an incoherent cocktail of modish philosophies and pseudoscience, adding a dash of unsavory racial theory for good measure.

Global influence: 20/100

Despite the claims of the Theosophical Society, it seems unlikely that initiation into its mysteries has done much to advance the cause of global peace. However, Theosophy has had immense cultural influence as the source of many New Age and Ariosophist (see page 53) beliefs and theories.

How to join

Visit the International Directory page of the Theosophical Society to find a branch in your area: www.ts-adyar.org/node/207.

Societas Rosicruciana

Related to the Freemasons, the Societas Rosicruciana had great influence on the development of esoteric secret societies, and today still instructs initiates in the mysteries of the occult.

Place of origin:	England
When:	1866
Founder(s):	Kenneth Mackenzie
	Robert Wentworth Little
Current status:	Active, USA

History

By Victorian times, Rosicrucianism had become a popular strand of occultism, offering the allure of magic with the reassurance of a solid Christian context. The profile of Rosicrucians was raised further by the success of *Zanoni*, the best-selling 1842 novel by Edward Bulwer-Lytton, which detailed the adventures of an immortal Rosicrucian adept, and included much convincingly authentic detail about the Rosicrucians.

It was against this background that the *Societas Rosicruciana in Anglia* (aka the Soc Ros or SRIA) was founded in 1866. The genesis legend of the SRIA is similar to that of other societies, for it supposedly came about when Robert Wentworth Little, who worked at Freemasons' Hall in London (the HQ of English Masonry), discovered a packet of papers in the vaults. With the help of Kenneth Mackenzie, an expert on Masonry and the occult, Little was able to decode the documents. They seemed to give instructions for setting up a Rosicrucian society, and handily Mackenzie had already been initiated into the German branch of this very group.

The two men structured the SRIA along similar lines to the OGRC (see page 41), with the same hierarchy leading from initiate to Magus. As in the OGRC, members had to be Master Masons, and were expected to pursue genuine studies in occultism. In 1871, the SRIA scored a coup by recruiting Edward Bulwer-Lytton himself as Grand Patron. Later the Society was led by William Wynn Westcott as Supreme Magus. Under Westcott the SRIA expanded into Scotland

and America (the Soc Ros in America and many other branches still exist today), and provided much of the inspiration for the Hermetic Order of the Golden Dawn (see page 48).

The conspiracy theories

If the tale of Little and Mackenzie is true, the SRIA represents the continuation of a mysterious and potentially ancient Rosicrucian lineage, with secret masters handing down their world-changing wisdom to a select band of initiates. Certainly the conspiracy community believes this to be the case, with the SRIA viewed as another tool of the Illuminati plot to bring about a New World Order, as well as perverting the minds of the impressionable by brainwashing them into occult/Satanic beliefs.

The skeptical view

The story of discovering a lost document, hidden deep in the archives, is just that: a story. This transparently fictional tale was clearly a ruse cooked up by Little and Mackenzie to lend bogus legitimacy to their desire to create a new club of their own, in which they could explore the occult while dressing themselves up with grand titles. The supposed antecedents of the SRIA are no more convincing than Blavatsky's Ascended Masters, while the recruitment of Bulwer-Lytton as Patron is a clue to the real inspiration behind the SRIA – a desire to cash in on the contemporary vogue for Rosicruciana. The supposed secret wisdom peddled by the SRIA and related societies is a vague mishmash of bogus history and navel-gazing esoterica.

Global influence: 9/100

Even the most credulous of observers can hardly claim that the SRIA has been instrumental in guiding human history, but it did have a real influence on the development of esoteric culture.

How to join

The American offshoot of the SRIA (which goes by the same initials) maintains a website at sria.org, and offers courses and links to like-minded societies.

Hermetic Order of the Golden Dawn

Though short-lived, this
occult secret society
achieved lasting notoriety
thanks to its illustrious
membership, influential
system of magic, and
plethora of splinter groups.

Place of origin:	England
When:	1887–1903
Founder(s):	Multiple
Current status:	Defunct

History

The Hermetic Order of the Golden Dawn (HOGD) was founded in 1887 by
William Westcott (a London coroner), Samuel Liddell MacGregor Mathers
(an eccentric occultist), and Dr. William Woodman, after Westcott found a
manuscript in cipher that apparently gave details of the structure and rites of a
magical organization. A new secret society was constructed along similar lines
to the SRIA (see page 46), but it lacked the credibility required to recruit new
members (specifically Masons). Fortunately, Westcott promptly uncovered
letters from a mysterious Fräulein Sprengel, head of a German order known
as *Die Goldene Dämmerung* (the Golden Dawn); once contacted, she
accommodatingly authorized Westcott to set up an English branch. Armed
with this license, Westcott and cofounders set up a temple of what they called
the Hermetic Order of the Golden Dawn, which they named the Isis-Urania
Temple, in reference to ancient goddesses linked to the practice of magic.

The society that Westcott and Mathers cooked up bore a strong resemblance
to the SRIA, with nine similar grades, although these were divided into three
orders: the First, or Outer Order; the Second Order, which included the grades
Adeptus Minor, Adeptus Major, and Adeptus Exemptus; and a secret Third
Order. In a bizarre and confusing arrangement, Westcott, Woodman, and
Mathers held the rank of Adeptus Minor and claimed to be subject to the Secret
Chiefs of the order, who held the rank of Adeptus Exemptus, but were actually
none other than Westcott, Woodman, and Mathers themselves. As for the Third

Order, its members were said to be immaterial beings from the Astral Plane (another dimension of existence). Different levels of occult study were offered for each grade: astrology and tarot for the first grade; ritual magic, scrying, astral travel, and alchemy for the second.

The HOGD quickly grew to more than 100 members, founding further temples in Weston-Super-Mare, Bradford, and Edinburgh. Membership was open to both men and women (unusual for a quasi-Masonic order), and recruits included the poet W. B. Yeats, the actress Florence Farr, the author Arthur Machen, and the occultist A. E. Waite. Mathers developed elaborate systems of magic and ritual, at one point constructing a replica of the polygonal tomb of Christian Rosenkreutz legend. He became the head of the Order when Westcott resigned in 1897, but it was not long before internal disputes began to tear the HOGD apart. Matters came to a head when Mathers admitted an ambitious but unpopular young initiate named Aleister Crowley (see page 51) to the Second Order, against the wishes of other members. In 1903 the HOGD broke up amid recriminations, splintering into "daughter" societies including Alpha et Omega and Stella Matutina (see page 55).

The conspiracy theories

For conspiracy believers, the HOGD, like the OGRC and the Soc Ros before it, represents a link in a long chain of Rosicrucian initiation, stretching back to the shadowy origins of the brotherhood in Biblical times and beyond. For paranoid conspiracy theorists of a fundamentalist/extreme bent, the HOGD is probably the most visible and objectionable expression of the

Right Rosicrucian symbol of the Hermetic Order of the Golden Dawn.

dark conspiracy to undermine Christian civilization through the practice of black magic and the infection of society with Satanic beliefs and degenerate lifestyles. For instance, the HOGD served as the training academy for the most notorious black magician of recent history, Aleister Crowley, who in turn went on to spread his filth to America, Italy, and elsewhere, becoming a cult figure and underground antihero – a sort of poster boy for the Illuminati conspiracy. Meanwhile, the conspiracy theorists argue, the true architects of the global conspiracy were revealed by the admission that the Third Order of the HOGD was composed of trans-dimensional beings (i.e., Illuminati-bloodline aliens).

The skeptical view

The HOGD was not part of a centuries-old tradition, the skeptics retort: Westcott's cipher manuscript was almost certainly the work of Kenneth Mackenzie, the cocreator of the Soc Ros (see page 46). Fräulein Springel was entirely imaginary, her letters crude fakes in poor German, forged to lend spurious legitimacy to the pet project of Westcott and Mathers. The magic invented by Mathers and practiced by HOGD members may have had genuine psychological power, in the sense of affecting its practitioners, but there is no such thing as supernatural power. In conclusion, skeptics say that the HOGD represented little more than an exercise in fiction and theater by Mathers, combined with the dilettante dabbling of bohemians attracted by the exoticism of the occult.

Global influence: 20/100

The HOGD gets a reasonable score because of its tremendous cultural influence. Most subsequent representations/interpretations of magic, occultism, and even Satanism owe much to the HOGD.

How to join

The original HOGD is defunct, but various orders now bear the same title and claim kinship – visit, for instance, hogd.co.uk. The real mystery is how to gain admittance to the Third Order, which requires ascent to the Astral Plane.

Ordo Templi Orientis

Thanks to its association with Aleister Crowley, this quasi-Masonic German order practicing sex magic became one of the most notorious magical secret societies.

Place of origin:	Switzerland
When:	1905
Founder(s):	Carl Kellner
	Theodor Reuss
Current status:	Active, worldwide

History

The Ordo Templi Orientis (Order of Oriental Templars, a.k.a OTO) was founded in 1905, the brainchild of German journalist Theodor Reuss and Austrian industrialist Carl Kellner, who were both Masons and Theosophists with a shared interest in the occult and, specifically, in sex magic.

Reuss set up his first lodge near Switzerland's Monte Veritas, a sort of proto-hippy community. In 1912 he contacted Aleister Crowley, former member of the HOGD and founder of a small, short-lived magical society of his own, the *Argenteum Astrum* ("Silver Star"). Crowley was a charismatic and compelling figure. Immersed in study of the occult from a young age, he had traveled the world picking up ancient traditions and supernatural revelations regarding what he called "Thelemic doctrine."

Crowley had his own agenda, however, and the OTO soon split into rival camps. Followers of Reuss would later set up the long-lived and popular society AMORC (Ancient Mystical Order Rosae Crucis), while an acolyte of Crowley's, the pioneering rocket scientist Jack Parsons, ran a Californian branch known as the Agape Lodge. The fractious nature of OTO politics continued, with rivals battling in the courts for control of the Order's legacy, yet it remains one of the biggest and most active secret societies in its various modern incarnations.

The conspiracy theories

In the conspiracy theory version of history, the OTO was a tool of the wider Illuminati conspiracy to pervert popular culture and spread Satanic practices. More specifically there are contradictory and murky claims of OTO involvement in magical aspects of the Second World War and related history. According to one tale, Crowley was commissioned by British intelligence to perform a magical ceremony in Ashdown Forest in Sussex in 1941, which was responsible for the mysterious flight to Britain of Hitler's deputy, Rudolf Hess. Meanwhile in America, the involvement of Jack Parsons implies to some that the OTO magically contributed to the American rocket program, and by association ties the OTO to the occult counterpart of Operation Paperclip (the program to recruit Nazi rocket scientists), which saw Allied attempts to coopt Nazi black magic programs.

The skeptical view

Stories relating the OTO to wartime magical rites and postwar conspiracies are pure fantasy, say the skeptics. The Order was originally little more than a vehicle for the sex-magic fantasies of libidinous old men, and latterly served as a cash cow for Crowley, who was by then a drug addict desperate for funds.

Global influence: 17/100

Through its involvement with the crucibles of modern 20th-century counterculture at Monte Veritas and the Agape Lodge, and its wider cultural impact, the OTO arguably did play a role in creating and spreading counterculture ideas and practices.

How to join

Descendants of the original OTO still practice today, and information about membership can be obtained by visiting the website oto.org.

Right Occultist Aleister Crowley, ca. 1921.

Ordo Novi Templi

Representing the dark side of secret societies, groups such as this helped to ferment the racial and historical fantasies that underpinned Nazi ideology.

Place of origin:	Germany
When:	1907
Founder(s):	Jörg Lanz von Liebenfels
Current status:	Defunct

History

Beginning in the late 1850s, a number of concerns and ideas were coming together in the German-speaking world to create the ideology sometimes known as Ariosophy. Ariosophy was an esoteric take on German paganism, mysticism, and history, in which pre-Christian German runelore and related occult material was tangled up with anti-Semitism and a pan-historical fantasy pitting Aryans against degenerate subhuman races in an epic contest for survival and the fate of humanity. Ariosophists created a number of secret societies, foremost among them the *Ordo Novi Templi* (Order of New Templars, ONT).

The ONT was founded in 1907 by Jörg Lanz von Liebenfels, as a modern-day version of a medieval warrior-monk order with Aryan racial overtones. The Order was based in a castle and members were expected to follow a sort of monastic code. Progress in the order depended on passing tests of racial purity. Von Liebenfels was also behind the Guido von List Society, which promoted the work of a prominent German novelist important in the formulation of Ariosophy. In 1908 this Society in turn spawned a secret society, the Höhere Armanen-Orden (Higher Armanen Order), which was devoted to occult aspects of ancient German history.

The conspiracy theories

Ariosophy constructed a grand Plot Theory of history, in which, it was claimed, the dark degenerate races (aka the Jews) had always been engaged in a vast global conspiracy to destroy the Aryans. Their battle had been fought out across a prehistoric geography similar to that of Theosophy, including lost lands such as

Atlantis, Hyperborea (the uttermost north), and Thule, the mythical homeland of the Aryans. Some of these beliefs have been adopted by modern fringe and even mainstream conspiracy theorists, although the anti-Semitic elements have been more or less obscured. Von Liebenfels added more detail to this conspiracy narrative, claiming that the ancient mystery cults had tricked humans into breeding with perverted dwarfs to defile the Aryan bloodline and deny modern Aryans their occult gifts. The ONT founder also championed the ideas of German novelist Guido von List, who had concocted a version of ancient Teutonic history in which the German tribes had been led by a caste of Druid-like priest-kings called the Armanen. Supposedly, the Armanen had safeguarded the occult wisdom of the prehistoric Aryans, and had passed this knowledge on to the Templars and Freemasons.

The skeptical view

Lanz was a Cisterician monk defrocked for sexual transgressions; his noble suffix was invented to fit his aristocratic pretensions. The ONT was based on fictions about medieval orders and a perversion of religious discipline. More generally, Ariosophy is a fallacious mixture of utterly discredited pseudoscience and historical fantasy. Theories about lost lands such as Hyperborea and Atlantis were formulated before the concept of plate tectonics was understood, and the archeological and linguistic evidence adduced by the likes of von List was bogus, misinterpreted, and often entirely made up. The Armanen never existed, and to the extent that the Aryans were a genuine historical people, they bore no resemblance in origin or nature to Ariosophist fantasies.

Global influence: 25/100

The ONT was an influence on the ideas of Hitler (not a member but an avid reader of its journal) and probably a direct inspiration for aspects of the SS (the *Schutzstaffel*, the Nazi party's paramilitary wing).

How to join

First ensure that all the ancestors you have ever had belong to an unbroken line of descent from fictional Aryan forefathers who dwelled in a nonexistent land. Now buy a castle and recruit similar delusional fascists to join you.

Alpha et Omega and Stella Matutina

Rival secret societies, each claiming to be the one true inheritor of the HOGD legacy, these daughter societies of the Golden Dawn have had a complex and fractious relationship since their inception.

Place of origin:	England
When:	Early 20th century
Founder(s):	MacGregor Mathers
	Robert Felkin
Current status:	Active, worldwide

History

In 1903 the Hermetic Order of the Golden Dawn (HOGD) split into three groups after a series of disputes, including a sex scandal caused by con artists and a power struggle between MacGregor Mathers and London members over the initiation of Aleister Crowley (see page 49). A faction under Arthur Edward Waite, who wished to focus on Christian mysticism rather than magic, split off to form the Holy Order of the Golden Dawn. Mathers and a group of loyalists soldiered on, calling themselves the Alpha et Omega (A+O). Mather's opponents styled themselves the Stella Matutina (Order of the Morning Star); led by Robert Felkin they continued to practice Golden Dawn ritual magic.

Mathers died in 1918, after which the A+O was led by his widow, Moina Mathers. Important members of the A+O included the occultist Dion Fortune, who would go on to found the Fraternity of the Inner Light and become probably the foremost occult practitioner in England, and Paul Foster Case, who left to found the Builders of the Adytum. The A+O effectively petered out on the death of Moina Mathers in 1928.

Meanwhile, the Stella Matutina struggled to survive the emigration of Felkin to New Zealand in 1916, except in that country where a temple continued to function into the 1970s. Its most significant recruit was Israel Regardie, a member from 1933 to 1934, who published the complete rituals of the HOGD starting in 1937. While this made available to the wider world the secrets of the Golden Dawn, it also helped to kill off both A+O and Stella Matutina in their original forms. Battles between those claiming to have inherited the mantles of A+O and Stella Matutina continue to this day.

The conspiracy theories

For conspiracy theorists, one of the enduring mysteries about the HOGD and A+O is the matter of the Secret Chiefs. Mathers claimed that they were part of the A+O setup, and as late as 2002 the leaders of the present-day A+O claimed to have been contacted by the Secret Chiefs, who supposedly passed on to them the secrets of the Third Grade. For paranoiacs this is clear evidence that shadowy Illuminati figures are still pulling the strings of HOGD-related societies even today. According to some, Dion Fortune and her A+O spinoff group, the Fraternity of the Inner Light, spent the Second World War engaged in magical rites to protect Britain and counteract Nazi occult actions. According to Fortune and many conspiracy believers, this magical Battle of Britain helped turn the tide of war.

The skeptical view

For skeptics, the proliferation of HOGD splinter groups demonstrates that secret societies have less to do with eternal truths and much more to do with power games and personal aggrandisement. Meanwhile, claims regarding Fortune's magical wartime contribution are baseless because, skeptics say, there is no such thing as magic.

Global influence: 18/100

Although claims of magical warfare can probably be disregarded, figures like Fortune and Regardie had considerable cultural impact through their popularization of magic and the occult.

How to join

Modern incarnations of both the O+A and the Stella Matutina can be accessed on the web – see, for instance, the Sanctuary of Ma'at at ritual-magic.com.

Opposite MacGregor Mathers (1854–1918) dressed to perform a magical rite, in a costume of his own design.

Thule Society

The secret society that gave birth to the Nazi party has been linked to conspiracies surrounding Himmler, the SS, and black magic.

Place of origin:	Germany
When:	1917–1933
Founder(s):	Rudolf von Sebottendorf
Current status:	Defunct

History

The ONT (see page 53) was not the only Ariosophist secret society. Founded in 1912, the *Germanenorden* ("Order of Germans") shared similarly outlandish beliefs about the nature and origin of the Aryans and their enemies, with an extreme right-wing political aspect. In 1917 Rudolf von Sebottendorf set up the *Thule-Gesellschaft*, or Thule Society, named after the mythical homeland of the Aryan people, as a Munich lodge of the *Germanenorden* (although its true origin was concealed). The Society was allegedly a scholarly study group, but amid the chaos of postwar Bavaria it was instrumental in raising a militia force – the *Kampfbund Thule* – to oppose Communists.

In 1919 members of the Thule Society set up a political party, and in 1920, under the influence of its new recruit, Adolf Hitler, this party became the National Socialist German Workers Party – the Nazis. Leading Thule Society members funded and mentored Hitler, while the *Kampfbund Thule* militia became the Nazi's paramilitary arm, aka the *Sturm-Abteilung* (the SA, better known as the Brown Shirts). When the Nazis came to power they shut down all secret societies, including Ariosophist ones, although organizations like the SS shared many characteristics with and took direct inspiration from societies like the ONT. Meanwhile, the SA was destroyed on the instigation of the head of the SS, Heinrich Himmler.

The conspiracy theories

In the conspiracy version of history, the Thule Society provided more than just the political and ideological underpinnings of the Nazis. As the conduits for a tradition of magical lore and occult wisdom, the Thule Society tutored Hitler and his Nazis in the occult (magical influence would help to explain Hitler's phenomenal rise to power). The link between the Nazis and this occult context has provided the jumping-off point for an elaborate mythology of Nazi occultism, culminating in the full-blown science fantasies of the Vril Society (see page 62). Specifically, the occult pursuits of the Thule Society and the ONT are said to have been continued by Himmler, for whom the SS constituted a neo-Templar-style order of racially and psychically superior warrior-magi. Himmler set up three SS departments for investigation of the occult, Ariosophy, and pagan religion, including the notorious Ahnenerbe (Ancestral Heritage Research and Education Society), which supposedly gathered occult wisdom and magical artifacts (such as the Holy Grail and the Spear of Destiny) via expeditions to Tibet, the Poles, Cathar-country, and elsewhere. Conspiracy paranoiacs believe the original Thule Society lives on, gestating occult Nazi plots for world domination.

The skeptical view

It is true that the Nazi party and Hitler owed much to the Thule Society, but the occult aspects of Ariosophy were delusions based on bogus versions of evolution and anthropology, and flimsy historical fantasies. There was no such place as Thule and there are no such things as psychic superpowers, skeptics say. Hitler may have drawn inspiration from Ariosophy, but there is no evidence he was interested in the occult. Himmler probably was duped by the occult aspects of Ariosophy, but the only thing his Ahnenerbe ever produced was dead-end pseudoscience.

Global influence: 40/100

The Thule Society scores highly purely on a historical basis: for its direct role in creating the Nazis, rather than any fantasies about its continued existence.

How to join

Acquire the Spear of Destiny or the Holy Grail. Shortly thereafter, you will be contacted by remnant Thule Society occultists.

Druids

Modern secret societies claim to have preserved the prehistoric traditions of the Druids, the priestly caste of the ancient Celts.

Place of origin:	Unknown
When:	ca. 50 BCE
Founder(s):	Unknown
Current status:	Defunct

History

Little is known about the original Druids, who played an important role in the society and culture of the ancient peoples of Britain, Ireland, and France around the time of the Roman conquest. What can be gleaned from ancient sources is that Druids formed a caste that combined priestly, educational, and judicial functions. They performed sacred rites and were required to undergo exhaustive, decades-long initiation and instruction. Their lore and teachings were exclusively oral, which helps to account for the mystery that surrounds them.

The next historical record of a group claiming to be Druids dates to the early 18th century, when the radical Irish philosopher and religious rabble-rouser, John Toland, adopted the name for a society he founded to advance his pantheistic beliefs. Around the same time, the pioneering antiquarian William Stukeley started calling himself a Druid, founding an order called Mount Haemus Grove. In 1781, the Ancient Order of the Druids (AOD) was founded in London, and half a dozen other Druid-associated societies sprang up over the next century or so.

The conspiracy theories

According to one school of thought, Druidism is Gnostic-inflected goddess and nature worship that was forced underground to survive a millennia-long war with the patriarchal power of the Church. Modern Druidic societies, such as the AOD, claim to trace their lineage back through Stukeley's Grove and Toland's Druids to secret medieval Druid societies, which themselves link back to the last pagans of 9th-century Scotland. Supposedly, they represent the continuation of the ancient, pagan tradition, with links all the way back to the mysteries of Stonehenge and the megalithic culture of Neolithic Europe. For conspiracy theorists less sympathetic to Druidism, the Druids were the ancient Illuminati alien elite, who went underground but have reappeared in the modern era to promote their anti-Christian Satanism under cover of an eco-hippie ethos.

The skeptical view

The original Druids are one of the least-known and most misrepresented groups in the whole of ancient history. Toland, Stukeley, and subsequent societies were part of an 18th- and 19th-century movement called the Druid Revival, which had no link to actual Druids. Claims that latterday neopagans have any continuous chain of association with ancient Druids are completely unfounded and have been repeatedly debunked.

Global influence: 19/100

The Druids were probably highly influential in pre-Roman Europe and helped marshal Celtic resistance to the conquest. Their latterday incarnations have had more modest influence as inspirations for the Green movement and elements of modern counterculture.

How to join

You can find the AOD on the internet. Alternatively, grow a beard and undergo a 20-year initiation, during which you will memorize millions of words of material in a purely oral context, and become expert in law, mythology, botany, medicine, magic, and religion.

Right Depiction of an Arch Druid in Judicial Robes.

Vril Society

A terrifying secret Nazi conspiracy to gain revenge on the free world using occult-energy-powered, reverse-engineered alien spacecraft, or fantastic fiction?

Place of origin:	Germany
When:	ca. 1871–1947
Founder(s):	Unknown
Current status:	Defunct

History

Edward Bulwer-Lytton's 1871 novel *The Coming Race* related the escapades of an engineer who tunnels into the Hollow Earth to discover a secret subterranean race of Atlantean survivors, who power their advanced technology (including flying machines) with an occult energy called vril. In the book, vril is described as "an electric fluid … capable of being raised and disciplined into the mightiest agency of all forms of matter." Some in the occult community took this seriously – could vril be a real energy force?

In Germany in 1930, the Reich Working Group on "The Coming Germany" published a pamphlet titled *Vril: The Primal Cosmic Power*, and another claiming to reveal Atlantean technology offering limitless energy supply, using a bisected apple as a symbol of the Earth's energy field. In a 1947 article, rocket engineer Willy Leys described a group he called the Truth Society, whose members sought mastery of vril by meditating on an apple cut in half.

The conspiracy theories

From these simple seeds a vast conspiracy narrative has grown, according to which the Reich Working Group was actually called the Vril Society. The Vril Society was set up by the Thule Society with ONT input, to develop and master technologies derived from ancient Atlantean technology of alien origin. SS-sponsored expeditions retrieved crashed flying saucers and other alien/Atlantean technology for the Vril Society, and brought it back to Himmler's Wewelsburg headquarters, a gloomy castle where all manner of unspeakable occult experiments and atrocities were perpetrated. Here the Vril Society reverse engineered the alien technology and were on the verge of producing a raft of super-weapons that would have turned the tide of war when the Allies invaded and swept away the Third Reich. Through Operation Paperclip and its occult parallels, the Allies sought to get their hands on this vril-powered technology, but SS escapees and key Vril Society leaders escaped to secret Nazi bases in Antarctica. There, in vast underground complexes (possibly connecting to the subterranean world of the Hollow Earth, with its Atlantean denizens), they have constructed a fleet of vril-powered saucers that will shortly issue forth and conquer the globe.

The skeptical view

If the above reads like the script of a science-fiction movie or computer game, this is because it is – several movies and games are based on this ludicrous fiction. Leys' Truth Society, actually the Reich Working Group, was a tiny and short-lived group. It was not called the Vril Society, and its entire output consisted of the two publications mentioned above. There is no record of it having any involvement with the Thule Society or the SS. Vril does not and has never existed outside the imagination of Bulwer-Lytton. Himmler did play at occult dress-up in Wewelsburg castle, but this says more about his delusional fantasy life than reality. Wild tales about Nazi survival and underground bases are not simply harmless fictions, however, as they inspire neo-Nazi movements to this day.

Global influence: 8/100

For its enduring cultural influence, the fictional Vril Society scores more than zero, but it had no real impact on the pre- or post-war world.

How to join

Locate a vast hole in the Antarctic ice cap, descend and negotiate your way past genetically enhanced Nazi cyborg guards. Also meditate on a cut apple until you can control vril.

Part Three:
Religious Societies

Eleusinian Mysteries

The greatest mystery religion of the ancient world, the Eleusinian Mysteries seem to foreshadow many elements of modern secret societies. Were they,

Place of origin:	Ancient Greece
When:	700 BCE–393 CE
Founder(s):	Unkown
Current status:	Defunct

for instance, the direct progenitor of Masonry and the Illuminati?

History

The Eleusinian Mysteries were religious rites concerning the myth of Demeter and Persephone, celebrated annually at Eleusis, a sacred site near Athens. Initiates underwent ritual purification and joined in a ceremonial march to a great temple precinct, the Eleusinion, gathering in the Telesterion ("hall of initiation"), once the largest building in ancient Greece. Here the mysteries were revealed, offering transformative revelation to the initiates.

The myth at the heart of the mysteries told of the kidnap by Hades of Persephone, daughter of Demeter, goddess of crops and agriculture, and her eventual restoration to the world above. The Mysteries explored the themes of death and resurrection through ritual reenactments. Initiates wore symbolic tokens, such as wands of sacred plants, and were given a fermented drink. When they arrived at the Telesterion, the Hierophant (high priest) stood before them on the threshold of the Anaktoron, the innermost sanctum. At the climax of the ceremony something was revealed (apparently involving sacred objects brought out of a chest), which transported the initiates to an epiphany and freed them from fear of death. The precise details remain mysterious because initiates were sworn to secrecy.

Dating back to at least 700 BCE (and probably much earlier), the Mysteries were celebrated for more than a thousand years. At first they were restricted to Athenians, but later were opened to all Greek-speakers. Famous names among

Above Triptolemus on a winged chariot with Demeter, a scene of the Eleusinian Mysteries on an Ancient Greek krater, 460 BCE.

the initiates included Plato and the Roman emperor, Augustus. The cult was suppressed along with all other pagan religions by Theodosius in 393 CE.

The conspiracy theories

In the conspiracy-theory version of history, the revelation at the heart of the Mysteries was of a sinister occult nature, possibly representing a form of brainwashing/mind control by ancient Illuminati. One of the central tenets of this theory is that there is a direct line of transmission from the Mysteries to modern-day secret societies. Many adherents and critics of secret societies believe that occult wisdom was passed from the Mystery cults via Gnostic Christians to the Templars and Cathars, and thence to the Rosicrucians and Freemasons. In Dan Brown's *The Da Vinci Code* version of the story, this occult secret concerns goddess worship, pitting the esoteric tradition against the patriarchal forces of oppression – hence the suppression of the Mysteries when the Church gained control over the Roman Empire in the 4th century.

The skeptical view

There is no evidence for direct transmission between the Mysteries and later groups, whatever Masons and conspiracy theorists may say. In fact, the true nature of the Mysteries is still unknown, thanks to the oath of secrecy that seems to have been remarkably well observed. The revelatory experience at the heart of the cult probably owes more to stagecraft and psychoactive drugs (the fermented drink given to initiates may have included psychedelic ergot, for instance) than magic or the supernatural.

Global influence: 20/100

Although direct influence can be discounted, the Mysteries probably did provide the template for many aspects of modern secret societies; they also probably contributed elements to Christianity (see page 70).

How to join

If you speak Greek and have not murdered anyone, bathe in the Ilissos River near Athens in February and sacrifice a pig.

Mithraism

Involving the secret worship of a sun god in rock-hewn chapels, the cult of Mithras was a rival to Christianity and possibly the forebear of Freemasonry.

Place of origin:	Ancient Rome
When:	ca. 1st–5th century CE
Founder(s):	Mithras
Current status:	Defunct

History

In Zoroastrianism, the ancient religion of Persia, the supreme god of light, Ahura Mazda, battled constantly with the powers of darkness. Alongside him fought his son Mithra, who later became the preeminent sun god of the Achaemenid Persian dynasty (ca. 5th century BCE). Like many other eastern gods, Mithra was popular with the Romans and was brought back to Rome (probably by soldiers) as Mithras, the central figure of the Mithraic cult. Mithras was a powerful warrior and the ideal companion – virtues that appealed to the military. His cult became widespread around the 2nd century CE, with *mithraea* (Mithraic chapels) found from Rome to the borders of the Empire (where most of the legions were stationed).

The mythology of Mithras told how he sprang from a rock fully formed, and immediately engaged in a battle with a cosmic bull. The blood and marrow of the bull became the fruits of the earth, and the symbolism of this bull-slaying was central to Mithraism. Its iconography featured in the *mithraeum*, which was hewn from the rock to honor the god's beginnings, and a bull sacrifice was the main ritual. Only men could be initiated, and all members started off as equals, passing through seven grades of initiation: raven, griffin, warrior, lion, Persian, heliodromus (sun messenger), and father.

Mithraism shared many features with Christianity – Mithras was the divine son of God who became mortal to share the suffering of humanity and was born on December 25. His followers met in chapels to take a communion, in which bread and wine were transformed into marrow and blood. Mithras was a god of resurrection, and initiation into his cult was said to offer immortality.

Mithraism was suppressed by the Christian emperors and died out around the 5th century CE.

The conspiracy theories

According to conspiracy theorists, like the Eleusinian Mysteries (see page 66), Mithraism represented a tradition of occult wisdom at war with Christianity, which stole its central elements and then persecuted and suppressed it. In this version of history, the Christians hated Mithraism because it revealed the occult roots of their own religion, and they tried to destroy it to cover up this blasphemous secret. But they failed: the parallels between Mithraism and latter-day secret societies like the Freemasons (see page 10) and Skull and Bones (see page 18) are not merely a coincidence. The Masons are the direct descendants of Mithraism, meeting in lodges (equivalent to *mithraea*), where initiates sworn to secrecy start off as equals and progress through a hierarchy of ranks, enacting symbolic dramas and meditating on a sacred iconography.

The skeptical view

There is no evidence that any element of Mithraism survived to form any direct link with modern secret societies like the Masons. Ironically, the only form of Mithraic survival is via Christianity, which some might argue owes some sort of debt to the lost cult, or at least shares similar sources.

Global influence: 20/100

As a significant competitor of Christianity in the Roman Empire, Mithraism has had a lasting influence on world history.

How to join

Locate a *mithraeum*, or carve out your own, and paint a mural of Mithras and the bull-slaying behind the altar. Animal sacrifice being frowned upon, use a suitable substitute – such as a libation of beef stock – for Mithraic communion.

Knights Templar

Legendary medieval order of warrior-monks linked to the Holy Grail, foundation of Freemasonry, and discovery of America; did they really harbor great secrets?

Place of origin:	Jerusalem
When:	1119–1312
Founder(s):	Nine Christian knights
Current status:	Defunct

History

The order was founded in 1119 in Jerusalem when a group of nine knights vowed to protect pilgrims traveling across the Holy Land. Assigned quarters next to the former site of the Temple of Solomon, they called themselves the Poor Fellow Soldiers of Christ and of the Temple of Solomon, aka the Knights Templar. Thanks to influential supporters in Europe, the Templars quickly grew in numbers, wealth, and prestige, accruing lands, money, and power. But the loss of the Crusader kingdoms in the 13th century deprived them of their primary base and purpose, and they fell prey to the designs of the French king, Philip IV the Fair. After pressuring the Pope to grant him authority to act, Philip launched coordinated raids on Templars across France in 1307. Over the next few years, about 60 knights were executed, many after being tortured. The Templars were formally dissolved in 1312 and the last Grand Master, Jacques de Molay, was burned at the stake in 1314.

The conspiracy theories

One claim is that there were initially too few knights to fulfill their stated duty, so, the logic goes, the order must have been formed for other reasons. According to one popular story, they were deliberately quartered on the Temple Mound so that they could excavate old tunnels, leading to an amazing discovery (theories range from the Holy Grail and the Ark of the Covenant to lost gospels) that enabled them to grow wealthy and powerful almost overnight.

The Templars were also said to have developed heretical religious views, possibly through contact with the Assassins (see page 86), the esoteric Islamic sect of mystical warriors. According to this tale, the Assassins were guardians of Hermetic wisdom and they initiated the Templars into this Gnostic tradition. Indeed, the Templars were accused by their medieval interrogators of joining with the Muslims in a conspiracy to overthrow Christianity – a view shared by some fringe conspiracy theorists today.

According to *The Da Vinci Code*-school of alternative history, the Templars became guardians of Gnosticism and the secret at the heart of Christianity – i.e., the bloodline of Christ (see the Priory of Sion, page 74). According to their accusers, both medieval and more recent, the occult practices the Templars brought back from the Orient included worship of a demon named Baphomet.

Conspiracy theorists believe that the Templars survived their 14th-century suppression, spiriting away their treasure to Scotland, where they lived on. Under the aegis of the Sinclair family, the Templars supposedly discovered America centuries before Columbus, and created the Freemasons as a vehicle for their esoteric wisdom and occult secrets.

The skeptical view

Most of the conspiracy theories are speculation and fantasy. Medieval prosecutors typically accused heretics of crimes such as sodomy, witchcraft, and devil worship; in the case of the Templars they may have added collusion with the "enemy." Under torture some Templars may have admitted to these charges, but this does not lend them credibility. The charges relating to Baphomet probably derive from confusion over Templar use of a medieval term for Mohammed, and were cooked up into a lurid fantasy by the Austrian writer Joseph von Hammer-Purgstall, in his ludicrous 1818 book, *The Mystery of Baphomet Revealed*. The claim that the true mission of the first Templars was to excavate the Temple Mound is a fiction invented by one of the men behind the Solar Temple (see page 77). In practice, the nine knights, together with their retinues, would have formed a formidable party adequate for their stated role. The explosive growth of the Templars requires no special explanation, and can be put down to religious, social, and political currents of the period. There is no evidence that the Templars practiced Gnostic Christianity, or that they were initiated into anything by the Assassins. The story that the Templars thrived in Scotland under the Sinclairs is bogus – the Sinclairs did not found Freemasonry, and there is no evidence of any direct link between the Masons and Templars. Claims to the contrary are based on an 18th-century fiction intended to recruit sympathizers to the cause of the exiled British royals, the House of Stuart. The legend of a Templar discovering America is based on a medieval forgery. In summary, the Templars were not a secret society.

Global influence: 15/100

The Templars were important in the Middle Ages, but have no contemporary role beyond pulp fiction.

How to join

Only nobles can become brother knights, and must gift all their money and possessions to the order. Still want to join? Find a chapter house and get the other knights to grant you admission.

Above Early illustration of the Knights Templar, an order that formed one of the mainstays of the Crusader armies in the Holy Land.

Priory of Sion

According to popular culture, the Priory of Sion was the secret society behind all other secret societies; in reality it was a giant hoax.

Place of origin:	France
When:	1956–1989
Founder(s):	Pierre Plantard
Current status:	Fictional

History

After the collapse of Roman rule in Gaul, the region that is now France came under the aegis of the Merovingian dynasty of Frankish kings, who ruled from 481–751 until they were deposed by the Carolingian dynasty. The Abbey of Zion was a religious order based near Jerusalem during the Crusades, but it was destroyed in 1291. Beginning in 1896, Berenger Sauniere, the parish priest of Rennes-le-Chateau, a poor village in Languedoc in southern France, raised eyebrows by spending money lavishly. In 1956 a fraternity called the Priory of Sion was constituted in Annemasse in France. In 1967 it featured in French best-seller *L'Or de Rennes* ("The Treasure of Rennes"), and in 1982 it was central to the alternative historical best-seller *The Holy Blood and the Holy Grail*, whose themes were revisited in the global phenomenon that is Dan Brown's *The Da Vinci Code*, published in 2003.

The conspiracy theories

The man who set up the Priory of Sion in 1956 and cowrote *L'Or de Rennes* was Pierre Plantard. He claimed that the Priory was a super-secret society that had actually existed since the early Middle Ages, and had been set up to protect the Merovingian bloodline and work for the restoration of their dynasty as the true kings of France. The Templars, the Rosicrucians, and the Freemasons were all creations of the Priory, helping to maintain its secrets, which included the existence of a Merovingian tomb near Rennes. Sauniere had uncovered encrypted medieval parchments leading him to the tomb, and had used the information to blackmail the Bourbon dynasty and become rich. Plantard's tale was apparently backed up by the existence of the Rennes parchments, and by a dossier in the Bibliothèque Nationale in Paris that contained a list of the Nautonniers (Navigators, or Grand Masters) of the Priory, including Robert Fludd (see page 39), Johann Valentin Andreae (see page 40), Leonardo da Vinci, Isaac Newton, Victor Hugo, and Jean Cocteau, culminating in the last heir to the Merovingian crown, Plantard himself.

The Holy Blood and the Holy Grail claimed to have uncovered further layers of conspiracy. The secret guarded by the Priory was the Holy Grail, known in Latin as the San Graal, or more properly the Sang Réal ("holy blood") – that is, the bloodline of Christ. The Merovingian dynasty had been founded by the descendants of Christ, who had survived the crucifixion, moved to France with his wife Mary Magdalene, and had children. Seeking to suppress the truth about Christ and protect their authority, the Church had colluded with the Carolingians to depose the Merovingians and suppress the holy bloodline, but the Priory had fought a long battle to preserve the secret, deploying Templars, Rosicrucians, and Freemasons in a conspiracy to prepare for a theocratic revolution that would place a Merovingian-Nazarene divine king (Plantard) on the throne of a United Europe. In *The Da Vinci Code*, Dan Brown added yet more material, claiming that the Priory's role was to preserve the goddess-worshipping nature of early Christianity against the attacks of the Church and, specifically, Opus Dei.

The skeptical view

This elaborate narrative is based on hoaxes and fiction. Plantard was a Vichy collaborator and fascist with royalist fantasies (although his parents were both servants), part of a French neo-Templar scene that mixed quasi-Masonic fictions of lost medieval chivalry with anti-Semitism, reactionary politics, and a desire to restore the monarchy. After the war, Plantard spent time in jail, before setting up the Priory of Sion (in reality named after a nearby hill, and not connected in any way to the medieval Order) to agitate in local politics, and as a vehicle for his fantasies of royal descent. After another spell in jail for abuse of minors, he resurrected the Priory, forging documents that he smuggled into the Bibliothèque

Nationale to back up his claims, and collaborating on the *L'Or de Rennes* book to promote the tale. The mystery of Rennes itself was based on a hoax by Noël Corbu, who owned Sauniere's old villa and had cooked up the story to promote his restaurant. Plantard had met Corbu and seized on the fraud to bolster his own hoax, forging the encrypted "medieval" parchments. The amazing success of *The Holy Blood and the Holy Grail* led Plantard to make a final attempt to revive the Priory in 1989, but he foolishly became embroiled in a legal case and was forced to admit in court that the whole tale was an elaborate hoax. Plantard died in 2000, and despite the thorough debunking of his fraud the story was revitalized by Dan Brown, who claimed in a foreword to *The Da Vinci Code* that everything within it was true.

Global influence: 16/100

Despite being a gigantic fraud, the Priory of Sion has had great cultural impact. Its fictional versions have helped spread alternative interpretations of the history of Christianity and made places like Rennes into huge tourist attractions.

How to join

Employ genealogical research to prove your descent from the Merovingians (or simply forge a family tree and smuggle it into the Library of Congress). Alternatively, discover ancient secrets buried in the countryside near Rennes.

Right Façade of the Mary Magdalene church in Rennes-le-Château, France.

Order of the Solar Temple

Neo-Templar order that became infamous for the mass suicide and murder of its members, and which has also been implicated in the death of Princess Grace of Monaco.

Place of origin:	France
When:	1984
Founder(s):	Luc Jouret, Joseph di Mambro
Current status:	Defunct

History

The *Ordre du Temple Solaire* (OTS) was founded in 1984 by Luc Jouret and Joseph di Mambro, two men with complex histories of involvement in New Age movements and neo-Templar societies. Jouret, a Belgian doctor and homeopath who had been a successful lecturer on New Age healing, was briefly involved in a neo-Templar organization called the Renewed Order of the Temple (ROT), founded by a French fascist. Like many French neo-Templar groups, the ROT combined alternative history, fantasies of restoring medieval chivalry, and reactionary politics, in a similar style to the Ariosophist societies of pre-Nazi Germany (see page 53).

In 1984 Jouret was expelled from the ROT when he tried to take it over, and went on to create his own New Age secret society, Club Archédia, membership of which would form the basis for the OTS. That same year Jouret hooked up with Di Mambro, a French watchmaker and former member of AMORC (see page 51), founder of the Golden Way Foundation, a New Age forum where Jouret had lectured. The pair collaborated to create the OTS as a vehicle to combine their New Age and neo-Templar occultism.

Using Golden Dawn-style ceremonies and regalia (including swords, robes, and theatrical altars), the OTS conducted religious and occult rituals intended to hasten the advent of the New Age. Members were asked to donate large sums of money. By 1989 they had recruited over 400 members, but when membership declined and people began to ask for their money back, things went sour. Jouret began to preach that pollution would cause eco-Armageddon, but that the initiated could escape to a higher plane of being. In October 1994, 52 members and former members of the OTS were killed by murder or suicide in Canada and Switzerland, followed by 21 more deaths in 1995 and 1997, all in Canada.

The conspiracy theories

Neo-Templar secret societies in postwar Europe enjoyed a murky relationship with the secret state, according to certain conspiracy theorists. Their virulent anticommunist politics attracted unofficial support from Western intelligence services and they enjoyed covert funding and judicial protection as possible elements in Operation Stay Behind (see page 111). Possibly such support extended to the OTS, and questions have been raised about its funding, membership, and relations with the authorities.

More titillating is the tale of the involvement of Princess Grace of Monaco (Grace Kelly) with the OTS. According to the makers of a documentary on the secret society, the former head of security of the OTS and an acupuncturist who worked for the Order both claim that Princess Grace visited di Mambro at an OTS temple in the summer of 1982. Supposedly she engaged in an occult rite to confirm her as a priestess of the Order, following which she transferred 12 million Swiss francs to its Zurich account. Later she quarreled with di Mambro and threatened to expose him, but in September she was killed after a car accident in which she crashed off a mountainside and into the garden of another OTS member.

The skeptical view

The death of Princess Grace was no more than a tragic accident, and there is no evidence to back up claims she was involved with the OTS.

Global influence: 5/100

The OTS has potency as a symbol of what can happen when secret societies go bad.

How to join

Membership is discouraged because it can be detrimental to your life expectancy.

Opus Dei

A Catholic order open to ordinary people, Opus Dei has been accused of acting like a secret society and engaging in conspiracies to prop up fascist dictatorships.

Place of origin:	Spain
When:	1928
Founder(s):	Josemariá Escrivá de Balaguer
Current status:	Active, worldwide

History

In 1928 Spanish priest Josemariá Escrivá de Balaguer had a revelation about the role of work as a route to "saintliness," and founded Opus Dei ("God's work"). The lay order eventually became a personal prelature of the Pope, meaning it answers directly to the papacy and is exempt from local or national oversight or control. From Spain, Opus Dei spread to Latin America and around the world; today it has more than 80,000 members, the overwhelming majority of whom are lay people. Escrivá died in 1975 and was canonized in 2002.

There are four categories of membership of Opus Dei. Cooperators are not fully paid-up members, but are supportive of the aims and workings of the order. Supernumeraries are lay people who take vows and follow Opus Dei guidelines in their lives and work. Numeraries actually run the order, living in Opus Dei centers; either priests or lay people, they must have a degree, and they take vows of chastity, obedience, and poverty. Finally associate numeraries are less-educated people who work in Opus Dei centers doing the household and clerical tasks; they are generally women, and take similar vows to the numeraries.

The conspiracy theories

Conspiracy theorists claim that Opus Dei acts like a secret society, keeping its agenda and membership hidden and concealing its true face from the world. They accuse the order of seeking to infiltrate government, the judiciary, and business by recruiting highly placed professionals so that they can further the Opus Dei agenda, which, they say, is religiously fundamentalist, socially extremely conservative, and politically virulently anticommunist and quasi-fascist. Opus Dei members have included many politicians, judges, media barons, and corporate leaders, including British and Spanish cabinet members, U.S. Supreme Court judges, and a former director of the FBI.

In Franco's fascist Spain, Opus Dei became closely associated with the dictator's government, and was known as his Holy Mafia. The order supplied several members of his cabinet who oversaw the economic direction of Spain until the 1970s. In Latin America, Opus Dei members had strong links with a number of right-wing dictatorships and military juntas, and such associations continue to this day – Opus Dei is said by some to have been involved in Ecuador's 2000 military coup, and in a failed coup attempt against Venezuela's Hugo Chavez in 2003.

Opus Dei's agenda can be traced back to its founder, Josemaría Escrivá, a

controversial figure. According to conspiracy theorists, he was a rabid anticommunist thanks to his experiences in the Spanish civil war, and formed Opus Dei as a vehicle to advance his reactionary belief that society should return to a rigidly stratified feudal structure, where everyone knew his place and the Church maintained social order. He was also a pathological misogynist and an anti-Semite. Opus Dei reflects these values, opponents argue – associate numeraries are reduced to semi-slavery and routinely abused, while the order seeks to brainwash all its members

Left Statue of Josemaría Escrivá, founder of Opus Dei, at St. Peter's Basilica, Rome.

through techniques like mortification, including self-flagellation, and the wearing of the cilice (a barbed strap worn against the thigh).

Conspiracy theories also swirl around Opus Dei's relationship with the papacy. It is said to have recruited Pope John Paul II while he was still an archbishop, and earned special favor by brokering a secret loan to the anticommunist Polish union Solidarity. More shockingly, Opus Dei is said to have been involved in the financial scandals of the Vatican, in which the Vatican Bank was used to help launder Mafia funds and embezzle money. According to one story, Opus Dei engineered the Masonic-style murder of Roberto Calvi in London in 1982 (see page 11), as part of a power struggle with the Masonic lodge P2.

The skeptical view

Most of these accusations are unfair or untrue, defenders of Opus Dei claim. Escrivá was a respected and pious man – apparently holy enough to become a saint in record time. Opus Dei is not a secret society; it is open about its aims, which are simply to encourage people to follow good lives according to traditional values, and to find holiness through perfection of their work. Although mortification is used by a few members as an aid to devotion, the practice and Opus Dei in general have been given a bad press, they say, thanks to the distorted picture portrayed in Dan Brown's *The Da Vinci Code*, in which a murderous Opus Dei monk is the main villain. In fact, Opus Dei is not a monastic order, and thus has no monks. Nor is there evidence connecting Opus Dei as an organization to Vatican financial scandals or right-wing conspiracies.

Global influence: 25/100

Opus Dei members have and do exert significant influence on business and politics around the world, although not necessarily through conspiracies.

How to join

Catholic, rich, successful in your profession, and ready to follow some pretty tough guidelines on day-to-day living, not to mention handing over a lot of cash? You can sign a contract to become a supernumerary – see the Opus Dei website for more info.

The Leopard Society

Feared secret society of West Africa dating to the pre-colonial era, members of which were accused of shape-shifting, cannibalism, and ritual murder.

Place of origin:	Liberia
When:	Early 20th century
Founder(s):	Unknown
Current status:	Active, West Africa

History

Early European explorers visiting the West African coast met many different peoples. Among the most notorious were tribes from what is now Liberia, but used to be known as the Grain or Pepper Coast. As early as 1668, the Kru people of the Cape Palmas region were accused of cannibalism, while a 1743 map labels the coastline between Liberia and the Ivory Coast as the *Côte de Mal Gens* (Bad People Coast). When freed American slaves set up the Liberia colony, starting in 1821, they came into contact with a number of secret societies, which were a common feature of tribal life across West Africa. Most were benevolent or harmless, but societies named for totemic animals, including the Crocodile, Snake, and Leopard, had gruesome reputations. Leopard Society members were said to dress in leopard skins and wear razor-sharp steel claws on their fingers; more lurid accusations were common (see below). Similar societies were encountered by other colonial powers after Africa had been divided up in the late 19th century.

The Leopard Society came to western attention in the early 20th century thanks to a series of sensationalist accounts, including Sir Harry Johnston's 1906 *Liberia* and Graham Greene's 1936 *Journey Without Maps*. A flavor of these accounts is given by a 1914 article from the journal *African Affairs*: "The Human Leopard Society adds another terror to the Colony which has been branded with a notoriety that might be applied to all others on the West Coast of Africa, namely, 'The White Man's Grave.'" The article goes on to describe how cannibalism is merely an initiatory element of the Society's "dark and mysterious rites." Graham Greene put it more succinctly, recording that one of his guides told him simply: "these people bad, they chop men." Up until the 1950s, scores of ritual killings were blamed on the Leopard Society, after which such societies were said to have been suppressed.

Also known as the Leopard Society is the Ekpe, found in parts of Nigeria and Cameroon. It is a traditional network of secret societies that in historical times provided a unifying force between the trading settlements that made up Old Calabar (today part of Nigeria).

The conspiracy theories

The Leopard Societies of West Africa were accused of practicing a variety of gruesome black magic, and perpetrating vast numbers of ritual sacrifices. Members were said to gorge on the flesh of the sacrificial victims, and to be able literally to transform themselves into leopards thanks to shape-shifting magic.

The skeptical view

The leopard is considered a royal beast throughout West Africa and an obvious totemic symbol of power – it is not surprising that religious cults and secret societies should identify with it. Accusations of ritual murder and cannibalism may have been true, but they were also typical slurs used to denigrate rival tribes or aimed at groups antipathetic to the colonial authorities; the evidence to back them up often proves sketchy and anecdotal. Claims of lycanthropy and shape-shifting are pure fantasy.

Global influence: 11/100

Leopard Societies had enduring cultural and social influence throughout West Africa.

How to join

Do NOT don the skin of a leopard and use your steel claws to cut out and eat the heart of a suitable victim; instead simply visit ekpe.org.

Part Four:

Paramilitary and Political Societies

Assassins/Hashashin

Deadly medieval Islamic sect
led by a man who controlled
the minds of an army of secret
killers, or misunderstood
religious minority?

Place of origin:	Persia (Iran)
When:	ca. 1094
Founder(s):	Hasan i-Sabah
Current status:	Active, S. Asia (Khojas)

History

The Fatimids were a Shi'a Islamic dynasty that ruled much of the Arab world beginning in Cairo in the 11th century. Thanks to various schisms, their particular brand of Shi'a Islam was known as Ismaili, and a further schism in 1094, over the succession, led a small band supporting a child called Nizar to break away and flee Egypt. Led by a Persian convert called Hasan i-Sabah, these Nizari Ismailis made their way to the mountains of northern Persia and installed themselves in an old fortress known as Alamut.

From this base the Nizari Ismailis became notorious as the feared Hashashin, which became westernized to Assassins. Surviving the enmity of their neighbors, the Assassins gained control of fortresses in Syria, and later enjoyed mostly good relations with the nearby Crusader kingdoms. Alamut fell to the invading Mongols in 1256 and the Syrian Assassins were crushed by the Mamelukes in 1265, but the legend of the Assassins would only grow in the West. Although their strongholds had been destroyed, the Nizari lived on; today they are known as the Khojas, and are led by the Aga Khan.

The conspiracy theories

The Assassins' name reflects their use of hashish, the narcotic resin of the cannabis plant, which they used to brainwash their acolytes into becoming mindless killing machines – the origin of the Illuminati NWO's mind control technologies, conspiracy theorists claim. Several medieval writers, including Marco Polo, reported how the leader of the Assassins, known as the "Old Man of the Mountains," would abduct recruits and bring them to the mountain paradise of Alamut (beautiful gardens maintained by the Assassin's architectural

Above The "Old Man of the Mountain" demonstrating his control over his assassins by ordering two of them to commit suicide.

prowess). There they would be pleasured by beautiful women until they were dosed again and brought before the Old Man, who would promise them readmittance to Paradise if they died in his service. At the end of the initiation process, the Old Man would declare: "Nothing is true, everything is permitted."

With their legions of zombie killers, the Assassins formed what Joseph von Hammer-Purgstall called an "empire of conspirators … [determined to] undermine all religions and morality … [with their] doctrine of irreligion and immorality." Although their mountain fortress was destroyed by the Mongols, the Assassins had already passed on their occult secrets to the Templars, who in turn founded the Masons, Rosicrucians, and Illuminati, as revealed by the similarity between their hierarchies. Today the evil work of the Assassins continues through the use of modern mind-control techniques to help bring about the NWO. The Aga Khan, paranoiacs claim, is a leading member of the Illuminati bloodline elite.

The skeptical view

Skeptics say that the accusations and myths about the Assassins are all examples of "black legends" – lies made up to smear a group for political/ideological purposes. The name "Hashashin" is itself a smear – in Islam use of intoxicants is forbidden and unclean. In practice the Hashashin (who called themselves *ad-dawa al-jadida* – "the new doctrine") probably practiced strict abstinence. What is more, the known effects of hashish do not match the legends of the Assassins, whose drugs were said to give them desperate courage and maniacal obedience. Far from the evil brutes of popular myth, the Nizari were noted for their scholarship, great libraries, and mastery of hydrological engineering, enabling them to survive in hostile environments. While the Nizari probably did have contact with the Templars, there is no evidence they influenced or passed anything on to them. More generally, the exotic and fantastic tales of the Assassins reveal more about Western Orientalism, a caricatured version of the East that came into vogue in the 19th century (see page 43).

Global influence: 19/100

In their day, the Assassins were a genuine force in the complex politics of the medieval Middle East, and their cultural influence has been enduring, both in reality, thanks to the Khojas, and in fiction, thanks to the legends of the Assassins.

How to join

The Old Man of the Mountains was known for kidnapping the fiercest guards from caravans traveling through the mountains, so brush up on your military skills and secure employment as a security guard with a trader in northern Iran.

Club des Haschischin

A group of artists, writers, and other bohemians in 19th-century Paris who met under the aegis of a mysterious Doctor X and modeled themselves on the Assassins.

Place of origin:	France
When:	ca. 1845–1849
Founder(s):	Jacques-Joseph Moreau de Tours
Current status:	Defunct

History

Jacques-Joseph Moreau de Tours was a French physician and early practitioner of psychiatry. He was also an intrepid traveler and pioneering anthropologist, who spent three years in Egypt researching drug culture. On his return to Paris he published a monograph, *Hashish and Mental Illness* (1845). At around the same time, artists and journalists began to visit a suite at the Hotel Pimodan, decked out in Oriental splendor. Here a mysterious man in Turkish robes, known as Doctor X or the Sheikh of the Assassins, would offer them a green paste that induced nightmarish visions and euphoric ecstasies. This outfit was known as the Club des Haschischin or the Order of Assassins, and members included many leading names from the bohemian world of arts and letters, including Théophile Gautier, Alexandre Dumas, Honoré de Balzac, and Charles Baudelaire. Dumas would immortalize his experiences at the Club by including them in fictionalized form in his novel *The Count of Monte Cristo*, in which the Count, much like Doctor X, doses the hero with a strange green paste that sends him on a wild ride. The Club soon moved on from the Hotel Pimodan and is thought to have disbanded in 1849.

The conspiracy theories

According to conspiracy theorists, the Club des Haschischin was a direct descendant of the original Assassins. Doctor X – obviously Moreau – was a latterday Man of the Mountains, continuing his predecessor's experiments in mind control via psychedelic drugs, using dark occult lore he had picked up in Egypt. Evidently Moreau had encountered some underground remnant of the original Assassins, still operating in Egypt. The psychedelic agent that Moreau dispensed cannot have been cannabis, which has a mild euphoric effect, but it must have been something much more potent; perhaps an artificial toxin manufactured with advanced Illuminati technology.

The Club, conspiracy theorists say, was a key element in the ongoing Illuminati plot to infect society with counter-cultural degeneracy. It presented all the elements of pernicious modern youth/counter-culture in prototypical form: the dangerous allure of drugs; antiheroes from the margins of society; psychedelic gurus spouting cod philosophy; and moral and sexual licentiousness.

The skeptical view

There is not a shred of evidence to link the original Assassins to the Club des Haschischin, skeptics point out. There may be some truth to the suggestion that Moreau viewed the Club as a vehicle for experimentation on his guests/test subjects, because he was engaged in an ongoing exploration of the physiology and psychology of hashish. Claims that hashish could not have been the drug are mistaken. In Egypt, where Moreau had studied the use of hashish, it was taken as *dawamesc*, a paste of highly concentrated cannabis containing massive doses of tetrahydrocannabinol, the active ingredient, and eaten rather than smoked. Ingested at such high doses, hashish can cause vivid hallucinations over long periods of time. Moreau adopted Oriental décor to help set his guests at ease, and probably to make the whole business a bit more fun.

Global influence: 10/100

The Club des Haschischin probably has had lasting cultural influence as a counter-cultural model, albeit not as part of an Illuminati plot.

How to join

Find a country where hashish use is legal (or at least decriminalized) and, together with various bohemian artists, befriend an eccentric doctor with an interest in psychedelics. You are now ready to start your own Club.

Ninja

The ninja are said to be
stealth warriors highly
trained in martial arts and
deception techniques, but
could they simply be an
invention, with no more
reality than Robin Hood?

Place of origin:	Japan
When:	ca. 17th century
Founder(s):	Unkown
Current status:	Defunct

History

The first unequivocal appearance of the ninja is in the literature and arts of Japan's Edo period (17th to late 19th century), specifically in the cultural movement known as the "floating world." This movement sought to supply content in a variety of media for an ossifying upper class and emerging middle class, and led to the emergence of mass-market prints, novels of incident and intrigue, and new forms of theater like *kabuki*. The ninja featured in all of these, a character or type signified by his outfit (black from his soft shoes to his cowl or hood), his role (in espionage and assassination), his techniques (the martial art known as ninjutsu), and his status (in opposition to the overt and honorable samurai, the ninja was covert and used any means necessary to achieve his ends). The Edo period also saw the first appearance of ninja "handbooks" – guides to the techniques and technology of the ninja.

Ninja really became famous thanks to two ninja crazes in the 1960s and 1980s, sparked off by blockbuster movies that spawned droves of "ninja-sploitation" imitations, such as *You Only Live Twice* (1964) and *Enter the Ninja* (1981). Starting in the 1980s the practice of ninjutsu also spread to the West, with martial arts enthusiasts studying with leading Japanese practitioners.

The conspiracy theories

According to modern-day ninjutsu enthusiasts and most popular literature on the ninja, they were a secret order of stealth warriors with roots in early-medieval

Japan, or even earlier. Masaaki Hatsumi, the preeminent modern ninjutsu practitioner, claims that: "the history of the ninja is long and ancient. Some say it extends back for more than 2,500 years, but in fact there are records going back as far as 4,300 years." According to folklore, the first ninja were taught their skills by the Tengu, mythical bird-man creatures famed for their ferocity and swordsmanship. Some modern conspiracy theorists see legends of the Tengu as folk memories of Illuminati aliens.

Mythical creatures aside, the origin of ninjutsu is attributed to monks and warriors forced out of China after the collapse of the Tang dynasty in the 10th century. The tradition they transmitted could be traced back to the physical and esoteric skills developed by ancient Indian priests, which Theosophists (see page 43) in turn trace back to Aryan root races and the Ascended Masters of Tibet.

Supposedly, these Chinese immigrants gravitated toward the rugged, mountainous provinces of Iga and Koga, bandit country similar to the Sicilian highlands, where poor communities developed strong traditions of self-reliance and self-defense against aggressive outsiders. Ninja clans, or *ryu*, developed their art until they became skilled stealth warriors, capable of sneaking into the most heavily guarded castles and assassinating warlords. Ninja were said to

Right Woodcut depicting a ninja, ca. 19th century, Japan (Ninja Museum, Uemo).

possess magical abilities, such as flight and invisibility, and manuals listed fantastical technology including tanks, submarines, flame-throwers disguised as cows, human cannonballs, Ferris-wheel-like siege-engines, hang-gliders, and water-spider shoes for walking on water.

In medieval Japan, ninja clans hired out their services to rival warlords, while during the more stable Edo period they were employed by the Shogun as a cadre of elite troops and later as his espionage agents. The last recorded mission of the ninja was said to be the infiltration of the ships of the American Commodore Perry in 1853, but their traditions and lore were passed on in secret in documents like the *Tora no Maki* (Tiger Scrolls).

The skeptical view

The ninja never existed, argue skeptics; they are entirely fictitious, a construct of "floating world" culture. Pre-Edo sources never mention ninja in the modern sense of the word, merely referring to spies, assassins, scouts, and so on. The "historical" characters famous as ninja today are folk heroes whose identities have mutated to fit cultural fads – originally they were identified as samurai or bandits. The classic iconography of the black-clad ninja, which does not appear before 1802, derives from the *kurogo* stagehands of *kabuki* theater – clad in black so as to blend in to the background, they became synonymous with stealth and invisibility. Ninjutsu-enthusiasts invented a complex history for their art, retrospectively recruiting characters and events that had nothing to do with the ninja. The Tiger Scrolls are bogus, say the doubters, and the ninja *ryu* are inventions.

Global influence: 6/100

Since they probably never existed, the ninja cannot be said to have had much influence on history, but the cultural impact of the concept is indisputable.

How to join

Several famous ninja were selected for instruction by ninjutsu masters after being spied fencing with trees (thus demonstrating their aptitude) – so travel to Iga province in Japan and start fighting the shrubbery.

Sons of Liberty

Originally a secret society agitating for American liberties and self-rule, the name was later appropriated by Peace Democrats during the Civil War.

Place of origin:	USA
When:	1765–1783
Founder(s):	The Loyal Nine
Current status:	Defunct

History

Appearing in Boston in 1765, the first Sons of Liberty group was set up by a small gang of lower-middle class artisans and merchants calling themselves the Loyal Nine, intent on resisting the imposition of the Stamp Act. Other groups sprang up in New York and across the 13 colonies.

As opposition to the Stamp Act increased, so did the reach and activity of the Sons of Liberty. In 1765, for instance, a mob composed of Sons of Liberty extremists rioted in New York, attacking the property of British officials. In Boston, a mob hanged and burned an effigy of the official in charge of enforcing the Stamp Act, and went on the rampage. British loyalists were liable to be tarred and feathered.

The repeal of the Stamp Act in 1766 saw the movement dissolved, but further unpopular legislation enacted in 1768 led to it being reconstituted. It remained active until 1783 when the Treaty of Paris officially recognized the existence of an independent United States. Its most notorious action was the Boston Tea Party protest of 1773.

In 1863, during the Civil War, a new group bearing the same name was set up by Peace Democrats (northern Democrats opposed to Republican conduct of the war against the Southern Confederacy). In 1864 a number of Sons were arrested and convicted of fomenting conspiracies against the Union.

The conspiracy theories

British loyalists during the Revolutionary War period viewed the Sons of Liberty as a well planned conspiracy to push the dispute over taxation into open revolution, while at the same time seeing the society as little more than a mob intent on looting the property of Loyalists. Since the Sons included many Masons, it has also been seen as a front for a Masonic conspiracy to foment Revolution.

The Civil War Sons of Liberty were painted as seditious traitors by Union Republicans, who called them Copperheads (after the venomous snake). They were accused of being fifth columnists, and of involvement in plots including the Northwest Confederacy (an attempt to form a breakaway confederacy of Midwestern states that would stay out of the war) and the Camp Douglas Rising (an attempt to free Confederate prisoners held in Chicago and other Midwestern camps).

The skeptical view

The original Sons of Liberty was not a monolithic conspiracy but a loose affiliation of groups from different cities and states, many of which originally had different names. Local chapters may have corresponded to coordinate policy, but there was no central command, say the skeptics. The Sons were narrowly focused on resistance to the Stamp Act, they argue, and there was no wider agenda or advance plan for independence.

The Civil War Sons were never the threat they were claimed to be. Their primary concerns were civil rights violations by what they saw as a dangerous dictatorial Republican regime. Republican politicians used *agents provocateur* and informants to develop trumped-up charges against rival candidates during an election year. The Northwest Confederacy and Camp Douglas Rising conspiracies were largely bogus.

Global influence: 20/100

Probably unintentionally, the original Sons of Liberty would have enormous influence on the course of the Revolution, as the basis for the Committees of Correspondence.

How to join

Meet under the Liberty Tree in Boston, bearing an effigy of the colonial governor (or nearest equivalent).

Carbonari

Secret societies that planned and launched revolutions across Italy in the early 19th century, spreading to the rest of Europe where they were behind revolutions in France and Greece.

Place of origin:	Italy
When:	ca. mid 17th–mid 19th century
Founder(s):	Pierre Joseph Briot
Current status:	Defunct

History

Carbonari means "Charcoal Burners"; the first Charcoal Burners were the French Charbonnerie, a fraternal association founded during the French Revolution, based on a co-Masonic society founded in Paris in the 1740s, known as the Order of Woodcutters. La Charbonnerie were primarily a social organization practicing Masonic rituals and teachings. Napoleon had conquered the various Italian states, incorporating some directly into his empire and making others dependent states. In Naples, for instance, Napoleon's brother Joseph was made king. Among the French in Naples was an initiate of La Charbonnerie, Pierre Joseph Briot, an old revolutionary who held to his fervent republican ideals. Seeking to counter the developing imperialism of Napoleon, Briot devised an Italian version of the secret society, the Carbonari.

Although the Carbonari shared many elements with Masonry, such as an elaborate Legend of Perpetuation, degrees of initiation, and division into lodges (known as *venditas*, or shops), there were important differences. *Venditas* in different areas were only loosely affiliated, making the organization difficult to suppress because it had no central body. In place of Masonry's esoteric symbolism and vocabulary, the Carbonari used more conventional religious imagery, making it palatable to a wider range of people, especially in southern and eastern Europe. Recruitment focused on the middle classes, from which most junior military officers and government officials were drawn. Carbonari were required to be armed with a rifle, ammunition, and a dagger; this secret society meant business.

Tapping into rising liberal, republican, and nationalist sentiment, the Carbonari spread rapidly. In 1820 they staged a revolution in Naples, followed by uprisings in Sicily the same year, Piedmont in 1821, and France in 1822. All were ultimately crushed by royalist forces and Austrian armies, but spin-off Carbonari groups, known as *economias* (economies), spread revolution to other parts of Europe, including the successful Greek rising against Turkish rule (1821–1826), the Decembrist rising in Russia in 1824, and the 1830 revolution

Above Affiliation of a new member at a secret meeting of the Carbonari; a wood engraving based on a drawing by Ludwig Burger, 19th century.

in Paris. The leading Italian revolutionaries of the era, Filippo Buonarroti and Giuseppe Mazzini, were both Carbonari.

The conspiracy theories

According to the Plot Theory of history, the Carbonari were simply a front for Illuminated Masonry (see page 13), representing the most visible actions of the grand Illuminati conspiracy to topple all governments and religion. Under the guise of republican ideals, they attempted to spread atheism and anarchy, so that the Illuminati elite could impose despotic rule over the remnants of society.

The skeptical view

Although they almost certainly derived from co-Masonic groups and took much of their apparatus from Masonry, the Carbonari were very different from the Freemasons. In fact, the great divergence between the passive, self-development and fraternal support nature of the Masons, and the active, revolutionary program of the Carbonari highlights the inaccurate and misleading nature of the charges often leveled at the Masons, skeptics say. The Carbonari prove that secret societies could plot revolutions (though with limited success) when minded to do so; the Freemasons proper eschewed direct political action.

Global influence: 36/100

Though most of their own uprisings were crushed, the Carbonari directly inspired successful revolutions in Greece and, later, in Italy.

How to join

Find a small state suffering under the yoke of dysfunctional royalist or oligarchic government, and swear mutual support with fellow Carbonari (known as "good cousins") over the blade of an ax.

Fenians

The Fenians, or the Irish Republican Brotherhood, were a 19th-century Irish-American secret society intent on securing Irish independence through force of arms.

Place of origin:	USA
When:	ca. 1858
Founder(s):	John O'Mahony
Current status:	Defunct

History

The horrors of the Irish famine of the 1840s fueled nationalist revolutionary sentiment in Ireland, leading to the Young Ireland movement and an abortive uprising in 1848. The leaders of the uprising fled abroad; James Stephens to exile in Paris, and John O'Mahony to America, where there were more than a million Irish émigrés. Stephens returned to Dublin where, in 1858, he founded a group of conspirators called the Brotherhood, bound by oath to support one another in their aim of driving out the British. Crucially, this Brotherhood, later known as the Irish Republican Brotherhood (IRB), could count on funds and armaments from their American branch, the Fenians or Fenian Brotherhood, named for the Fianna, a legendary band of warriors from Irish history. The Fenians were constituted in New York by John O'Mahony, and would also have branches in Australia and Britain.

The IRB was modeled on European secret societies like the Carbonari (see page 96), with strict rules to ensure security, such as operating in small cells, supposedly unknown to one another. Unfortunately, they were easy prey for British spies and informers, especially because their American branch, the Fenians, made little effort to avoid the limelight, running newspapers and organizing public meetings. In the 1860s an influx of Irish veterans of the American Civil War prompted ambitious plans to prepare assaults on two fronts.

In 1867, the IRB launched an insurrection in Ireland, intended to link up with troops and weapons arriving from America aboard the Fenian-funded ship,

Erin's Hope. The uprising was crushed by the time the ship landed, and its passengers were captured. Meanwhile, many American Fenians felt that Britain was more vulnerable in its North American territories, and in 1866 a small force of Fenians invaded Canada and captured Fort Erie, before being forced to withdraw. Further Fenian raids launched from Vermont in 1870 also failed.

Now discredited, the Fenians diminished, but their Irish wing regrouped, backing a terrorist campaign in Britain in the 1880s and coordinating with other Irish independence groups to launch the Easter Uprising of 1916. Although this too was crushed, it set in motion the revolution that would lead to an independent Ireland in 1921, led by IRB president Michael Collins.

The conspiracy theories

Proponents of the Plot Theory of history see the Fenians and the IRB as puppets of Illuminated Masonry, part of their global conspiracy to topple all governments and religions. They point to the obvious influence of the Carbonari on the Fenians, and extrapolate from this to the role of the Masons.

The skeptical view

The Carbonari probably did influence the Young Ireland movement, which in turn inspired the creation of the Fenians, but there is no evidence of any direct link, let alone a connection with the Freemasons. While it is true that the Fenians were initially opposed by the Catholic Church, skeptics argue that it is ridiculous to claim that they were atheists or antireligious. Far from being part of a super-secret global conspiracy, the Fenians were among the least secret of secret societies, which was a major problem for them.

Global influence: 20/100

The IRB were instrumental in securing an independent Ireland, albeit the Fenians were less successful in invading Canada.

How to join

Secret societies intent on using violence against the British in Ireland still exist, so membership of any relic Fenian group is no joking matter.

Molly Maguires

A secret society of Irish-American mine-workers in the coal fields of Pennsylvania in the 1870s, who were accused of perpetrating a series of murders.

Place of origin:	Ireland
When:	ca. 18th century
Founder(s):	Unkown
Current status:	Defunct

History

Appalling conditions in Ireland forced the emigration of more than a million Irish to America in the 19th century, but many found that their plight on arrival was little better. Irish miners coming to work in the coalmines of Pennsylvania suffered low wages and deadly conditions, and faced vicious anti-Irish sentiment from mine owners and other workers. During the 1860s there was a series of unsolved murders targeting mine owners, foremen, and local officials.

In 1869 an early form of trade union, the Workingmen's Benevolent Association (WBA), started to push mine owners for better pay and conditions. Around the same time, railroad magnate and mine-owner Franklin Gowen was consolidating his grip on the industry and in 1873 he employed a Pinkerton Agency detective, James McParlan, to infiltrate and uncover a secret terrorist organization of which he had heard rumors. Known as the Molly Maguires, they had supposedly formed under the cover of the quasi-Masonic Ancient Order of Hibernians (AOH), a fraternal society popular with Irish in America and Ireland.

McParlan claimed to have successfully infiltrated the Molly Maguires and linked them to a new series of murders targeting "enemies" of the Irish miners. In 1876 a string of arrests were made, and in trials over the next few years 20 alleged Molly Maguires were hanged, with others imprisoned.

The conspiracy theories

The story advanced by Gowen, with the help of McParlan's testimony and the backing of sympathetic newspapers, was that the Molly Maguires were a terrorist secret society straight from the old country. Supposedly, in Ireland in the 1840s, gangs of agitators dressed in women's clothes and blackened their faces to vandalize property and terrorize landlords, taking their name from a woman said to have been cruelly evicted. Under the cover of the AOH, a shadowy global conspiracy with tentacles reaching across the Atlantic, these criminals had brought their reign of terror to America, setting up the WBA as a cover for their lethal combination of socialist agitation and assassination.

The skeptical view

The story of the Molly Maguires is a tragic tale of racism and miscarriage of justice in the service of predatory capitalism. There is no evidence to suggest that Irish miners in Pennsylvania had brought any secret societies with them from the old country. In fact there is no real evidence that the Maguires even existed. The only testimony to that effect came from McParlan himself, a dubious character in the pay of Gowen, who featured as the star prosecutor in the case. The jury was picked to comprise German-Americans with poor English and ethnic enmity against the Irish, and the proceedings were a travesty of justice. Gowen used the episode to blacken the name of the AOH, a perfectly harmless organization, and to destroy the WBA, a legitimate union and a threat to his bottom line. If the Maguires did exist, they represented what the dispossessed, disenfranchised, and alienated Irish felt was the only means of political expression available to them; if there were parallels with previous events in Ireland it is hardly surprising given the similarity of the intolerable constraints imposed on the Irish in both cases.

Global influence: 15/100

Although the Molly Maguires, if they ever existed, had been suppressed, the unionization process they helped to start would soon bear fruit with the formation of the United Mine Workers of America in 1890.

How to join

Frequent bars in a company town where Irish workers are subjected to 19th-century labor conditions, pretend to be a member of the AOH, and mention that you own a dress.

The Boxers

The Society of Righteous and
Harmonious Fists, or Boxers,
was a secret society
practicing magic and martial
arts, which instigated a
rebellion against foreign
influence in China in 1900.

Place of origin:	China
When:	1898–1901
Founder(s):	Unknown
Current status:	Defunct

History

The late 19th century was a turbulent time in China: new technology such as steamboats and machinery had put many out of work, at a time when peasants and workers were suffering from floods and famine. Among these troubled masses there was a groundswell of revulsion for all things foreign, from technology to the hated missionaries and their converts, so-called "rice Christians." Tapping into these reactionary, populist sentiments was a new movement, the secret society *I-ho Chuan*, variously translated as the Society of Righteous and Harmonious Fists, or the Boxers, from the martial arts they practiced.

The Boxers had their roots in the Chinese tradition of sects that mixed magic, martial arts, and other physical components such as breathing techniques (see the Triads, page 124). In 1899 the Boxers appeared in the northern region of Shantung, growing out of two precursor societies, the Big Swords and the Spirit Boxers.

The Boxers destroyed telegraph lines, raided missions, and murdered missionaries and converts. They adopted the slogan "Support the Qing, exterminate the foreigners," and when in1900 the Boxer uprising reached Beijing, their forces were supplemented by Imperial troops. After a 55-day siege, an expeditionary force relieved the siege, massacred thousands of Chinese, and forced a harsh treaty on the humbled Qing dynasty. The Boxers had already been absorbed into the Imperial Army; most of them were killed or scattered.

The conspiracy theories

The Boxers spread wild conspiracy theories about foreign missionaries, claiming they harvested body parts from Chinese victims for their medicines, and created storms by fanning in the nude. The Boxers themselves were believed to have magical invulnerability, and to be possessed by spirits and gods. Such beliefs were used in turn by the foreign powers to justify their claims of racial superiority over what were depicted as the superstitious and deranged Chinese.

The skeptical view

The bizarre beliefs of the Boxers were a response to social, economic, and cultural trauma on a massive scale, but there was nothing uniquely Chinese about them. Similar wild beliefs were current then even in Europe. There is no substance to the claims of magical powers made by the Boxers. Commentators at the time noticed that during their demonstrations of supposed invulnerability, Boxers were often injured; such instances were explained away as "poor technique."

Global influence: 25/100

The Boxer uprising had profound consequences for China's development and Chinese attitudes to the West to this day.

How to join

Find a Boxer demonstration and join in by calling down one of the Taoist gods to possess you. Also practice breathing techniques until invulnerable to bullets.

Right French soldiers man a barricade on the French Bund in Tianjin, during the Boxer Rebellion, 1900.

Ku Klux Klan

Once the most feared American secret society, the Klan has been through several incarnations, preaching its doctrine of race hatred and reactionary violence.

Place of origin:	USA
When:	ca. 1860s
Founder(s):	Confederate veterans
Current status:	Active, mainly USA

History

Founded in 1865 by Confederate veterans, the Ku Klux Klan takes its name from the Greek word *kuklos*, meaning "circle," and the Scottish term *clan*. At first the Klan engaged in simple Halloween-style pranks, dressing up as goblins and ghosts, but in the era of the Reconstruction of the South, its secrecy was used as cover for violent racism. Under the leadership of Confederate general Nathan Bedford Forrest, the Klan grew explosively, and although it was modeled on military lines, it retained the terminology and costume of its earliest days. Forrest was the Grand Wizard, ruling over the Invisible Empire; beneath him were ranks such as Genie, Dragon, Hydra, Titan, and Goblin, ruling over areas known as Realms, Dominions, and Dens. The distinctive "ghost" costume was adapted from the outfits worn by 18th-century Irish secret militias such as the Whiteboys.

A campaign of violence and murder against African-Americans and Republican interests across the South brought down the wrath of the Federal Government, which managed to suppress the Klan, while the abandonment of Reconstruction and the introduction of legal segregation meant many of its aims were achieved. The success of the 1915 movie *Birth of a Nation*, which portrayed the Klan as heroes, led to its revival under William J. Simmons, who drew up new rituals for his Knights of the Ku Klux Klan in a book called the *Kloran*. Canny PR led to explosive growth, with membership rocketing from a few thousand in 1920 to more than 4 million by 1924. Aligning itself with Protestant fundamentalism, the Klan recruited thousands of church ministers. Attempts to translate popularity into public office backfired in 1925 when Indiana Grand Dragon David C. Stephenson, preparing to run for President, was arrested for kidnap and rape. The Klan collapsed outside its Southern heartlands, and declined further when it sided with the Nazis during the Second World War.

A postwar revival as the United Klans of America (UKA) coincided with the Civil Rights movement and the Klan grew once more, reaching a membership of 50,000. But the violence and terrorism employed by the Klan led to an FBI crackdown, while civil suits bankrupted many UKA groups. Since the 1980s the scattered remnants of the Klan have been closely affiliated with neo-Nazi groups and the militia movement.

The conspiracy theories

Conspiracy theories have been the lifeblood of the Klan since its inception, driving its growth and setting its agenda. In the Reconstruction era, the appeal of the Klan was based on conspiracy theories conflating the threat of economic and political domination by Northern Republican "carpetbaggers" with racism, through the lens of female sexuality. The Klan's hateful argument went that vengeful Republicans were intent on unleashing slavering hoards of animalistic blacks to pollute racial purity with widespread miscegenation, thus forever destroying the white South. The Klan claimed they were defenders of Southern womanhood, and through them of the South itself.

In its pan-American Prohibition-era incarnation, the Klan played on fears of Catholic and Jewish conspiracies to swamp Protestant America under a tide of superstitious immigrants. It was claimed that the nation's Catholics were stockpiling weapons to launch a coup under the direction of the Pope himself (aka "the Dago on the Tiber"), while a Jewish-Bolshevik conspiracy threatened the "honest" capitalism of small-town America.

In the 1930s the Klan set itself against the New Deal, making the link between communism and the federal government itself, as a threat to the American way of life. After the Second World War this hysterical anticommunism ramped up and was blended with anti-Semitism, so that the Civil Rights movement became a Jewish-Bolshevik conspiracy to mongrelize the races, thus enabling a communist takeover. In the 1970s, with the Nazification of the Klan, anti-Semitism became the overarching conspiracy driver, with the Zionist Occupying Government as the enemy, deploying feminism, the welfare state, gay rights, etc., as tools for destruction of the white race.

The skeptical view

Klan conspiracy theories have always been projections of the fears and insecurities of the white lower and middle classes, as they have struggled to come to terms with issues such as the economic decline of the South, demographic changes, multiculturalism, and the decline of the patriarchy.

Global influence: 35/100

The Klan have had enormous influence on government policy and national sentiment at times during their existence, and though the organization is currently fragmented, many of its habitual themes – such as the American way being threatened by immigration, non-Christians, culture wars, economic decline, and the federal government itself – loom large in current political discourse.

How to join

Unfortunately the Klan is still active so you could sign up, but because they hate everyone, the chances are that you fall into one of their designated "enemy" groups.

Above Ku Klux Klan rally, Maryland, 1986.

Black Hand

Serbian nationalist secret society formed in 1911 to advance the cause of Serbian expansionism through violence, responsible for the assassination that triggered the First World War.

Place of origin:	Serbia
When:	1911–1917
Founder(s):	Serbian army officers
Current status:	Defunct

History

Known to its own members as *Ujedinjenje ili smrt* ("Unification or death!"), but more widely known as *Crna ruka* ("the Black Hand"), this Serbian secret society was founded in Belgrade in 1911 by nine leading Serbian army officers. According to its constitution, its aim was: "To realize the national ideal, the unification of all Serbs. This organization prefers terrorist action to cultural activities; it will therefore remain secret." The Black Hand arose in response to tensions between the young nation of Serbia and its neighbor, the Austro-Hungarian Empire. In particular, Serbia was fiercely resentful of Austria's 1908 annexation of Bosnia-Herzegovina, territory that Serbs believed belonged to them.

The head of the Black Hand, codenamed APIS, is widely believed to have been Dragutin Dimitrijević, chief of the Intelligence Department of the Serbian General Staff. Under his guidance, the Black Hand formed numerous small cells of saboteurs, spies, and terrorists. They became influential in Serbian politics and launched daring missions, such as a failed 1911 attempt to assassinate Austrian emperor Franz Josef. By 1914, the Black Hand had 2,500 members and was believed to be closely involved with the government.

In 1914, Austrian Archduke Franz Ferdinand, heir to the Austro-Hungarian crown, agreed to visit Sarajevo, capital of Bosnia. This was seen by the Serbs as a provocation, especially since the trip was scheduled for June 28, a national day of remembrance. The assassination of the Archduke by a Bosnian Serb, Gavrilo Princip, enraged the Austrians, who in turn made intolerable demands on the

Above Italian newspaper illustration of the assassination of Archduke Franz Ferdinand of Austria, July 5, 1914.

Serbs. When these were rebuffed, the Austrians declared war, prompting Russia, Serbia's ally, to mobilize its armies. A domino chain of mobilizations in Germany, France, and eventually Britain followed, triggering the First World War. The conflict went badly for Serbia, and politicians blamed the Black Hand. Its leaders were arrested and APIS and three others were executed on June 26, 1917.

The conspiracy theories

The widely accepted conspiracy theory about the Black Hand is that they were responsible for the Archduke's assassination – they had armed Princip and six other terrorists, all of whom were either members of the Black Hand or an affiliated organization, Young Bosnia. What is more, the Black Hand operated at the behest of the Serbian government, itself a tool of the Russians. A more recent (and deranged) view, derived from the Plot Theory narrative, is that the Black Hand was an agent of the wider Illuminati conspiracy to destabilize established governments; the outbreak of the First World War was the ultimate realization of their dark plans.

The skeptical view

Princip probably was connected to the Black Hand, although he may not have been a member, but it is possible that the Serbian government knew nothing of the plot. The Black Hand represented the violent, militaristic faction of Serb nationalists, and there was tension between them and the more moderate governmental factions who wished to pursue more diplomatic means. Equally, there is no evidence that the Russians conspired in the assassination. Equating the reactionary, right-wing Black Hand with the supposed radical Illuminist conspiracy is simply fantasy born of the search for simplistic overarching explanations for events with complex and messy causation.

Global influence: 40/100

As direct triggers of the Great War, the Black Hand bear a potentially unique distinction among secret societies in terms of influence on the course of history.

How to join

Track down APIS (if one exists) and swear before him the following oath: "… before God, on my honor and my life, I will execute all missions and commands without question. I swear before God, on my honor and on my life, that I will take all the secrets of this organization into my grave with me."

Odessa and Gladio

Western European secret societies or operations, in which former Nazis formed anticommunist "Stay Behind" forces in case of Soviet invasion.

Place of origin:	West Germany
When:	ca. 1945
Founder(s):	Reinhard Gehlen
Current status:	Defunct

History

As the Second World War drew to a close, the Americans recruited Reinhard Gehlen, the Gestapo general at the head of the military intelligence agency responsible for the Eastern Front. Gehlen had already concluded that the war was lost and Hitler doomed, and carefully secured copies of all his files before turning himself over to the Americans, who sent him back to West Germany after the war as the head of the Gehlen Org, a secret society that later became the official West German intelligence agency. The Gehlen Org was responsible for providing the vast majority of NATO intelligence on Warsaw Pact countries, growing to employ 4,000 people, all bankrolled by the Americans.

Meanwhile, the CIA was desperate to guard against the very real threat of a Soviet invasion of Western Europe. Accordingly they set up a secret organization/operation, variously code-named the Allied Coordination Committee, Operation Stay Behind or Gladio (from the Latin for "sword"). Gladio recruited anticommunists (many of them Axis veterans) and funded and armed them so that they could form the nucleus of resistance to a Soviet invasion. Countries that have admitted its existence (including Belgium, France, Germany, Greece, Italy, Holland, Portugal, and Norway) say that its branches have been shut down.

The conspiracy theories

According to conspiracy theorists and many historians, the Gehlen Org and Gladio concealed a number of dirty secrets. For instance, it is claimed that working with the CIA, the Catholic Church, and others, they created the Odessa operation. Odessa was the German acronym for "organization of former SS members," and was tasked with protecting Nazi war criminals and smuggling them and their looted treasures to safety in Switzerland and South America via the so-called "ratlines." One tactic used by Gehlen (himself a war criminal) was to put former SS and Gestapo men on the payroll of the CIA by employing them in his Org.

The various Gladio secret societies, claim the conspiracy theorists, also carried out covert anticommunist activities across Western Europe, most notably in Italy, where they were responsible for the "strategy of tension." This was a program of fake left-wing terrorist outrages intended to discredit the communists and help install right-wing governments. Gladio operations are also said by some to have been behind the kidnap and murder of Italian Prime Minister Aldo Moro in 1978, and the Bologna train station terrorist bombing of 1980, both with the covert support of Italian secret services and the CIA. Gladio also had links to P2 (see page 113).

The skeptical view

Others claim that American recruitment of former German anticommunists was justified because of the threat posed by communism. Gehlen had convinced his American handlers he was not a fervent Nazi, and promised not to employ Nazis. Odessa was simply a fantasy, the skeptics say, created by novelists such as Frederick Forsyth (author of *The Odessa File*). Gladio did not extend to active operations, and Italian judicial investigations have not found conclusive evidence linking Gladio to the Moro murder or Bologna bombings, which were probably the work of left-wing terrorists.

Global influence: 35/100

It seems very likely that CIA-sponsored anticommunist secret societies have been the hidden hand behind some of postwar European history.

How to join

The threat of communist invasion has receded in Europe, so your best bet may be to set up a similar organization in regions threatened by Chinese expansion.

Propaganda Due

Propaganda Due was a secret Masonic lodge in Italy linked to Operation Gladio, South American dictators, Vatican-Mafia banking scandals, murder, and terrorism.

Place of origin:	Italy
When:	1877–1981
Founder(s):	Unknown
Current status:	Defunct

History

Propaganda Due (P2) was a secret lodge of Italian Masonry, formed in 1877 to get around the Catholic Church's prohibition on Freemasonry. Suppressed by Mussolini, it was revived in 1946. In 1967 Licio Gelli was made secretary of the lodge, and it is believed he set about recruiting a wide cross-section of the Italian elite, including politicians, military men, Mafiosi, and Vatican officials.

Little is known for certain of the activities of P2 until 1981, when authorities investigating the Banco Ambrosiano scandal raided Gelli's villa. Banco Ambrosiano (BA) had been Italy's largest private bank, but was implicated in massive financial crimes that included the disappearance of hundreds of millions of dollars from the Vatican Bank. The raid on the villa unearthed a list of 900 supposed members of P2, including the names of many prominent people. Italy was shocked, the government fell, and parliament passed a law banning secret societies, marking the end of P2. In 1982 Roberto Calvi, head of BA and a P2 member, was found hanging under London's Blackfriars Bridge with bricks in his pockets. At first ruled a suicide, his death was later deemed to be murder.

Gelli has avoided justice by repeatedly escaping the clutches of the authorities, first fleeing to Switzerland, then South America and France, despite being arrested and eventually sentenced to prison. A 1998 police search of his villa turned up 165 unmarked gold ingots buried in flowerpots.

The conspiracy theories

Conspiracy theorists and many mainstream commentators believe that Gelli and P2 were heavily involved in a breathtaking range of conspiracies. Immediately after the war, Gelli is believed to have been instrumental in setting up the ratlines, which helped smuggle Nazi war criminals to South America, with, some claim, CIA collusion (see Odessa/Gladio, page 111). Gelli grew rich and forged contacts that were instrumental to his role in helping set up Gladio operations, and by the time he took control of P2 his web of influence extended, it is claimed, from South American dictators and the CIA to the Mafia and the Vatican. P2 brokered major deals financing shady operations in Latin America, laundering Mafia and alleged CIA drug money, embezzling Vatican funds, and bankrolling anticommunist dictators and militia across the world. According to one story, Juan Perón, President of Argentina, knelt at Gelli's feet to thank him for his help in restoring him to power. As head of P2, Gelli was the only man who knew the complete membership; he was known as *Il Burattinaio*, the Puppet Master. When the secret service chiefs joined P2 they turned over to him all their files, allowing him to blackmail when persuasion and bribery failed.

In Italy P2 was said to be the guiding hand behind the "strategy of tension," overseeing the funding and arming of fascist cells masquerading as left-wing radicals, and ensuring that the authorities protected them and covered their trail. P2, the theory goes, was behind the 1978 kidnap and murder of Aldo Moro, who as prime minister was about to come to a historic accommodation with the Italian Communist Party, despite alleged American warnings that it might be

Above Three photos of Licio Gelli shown by his lawyers at a press conference, Rome, 1981.

dangerous to his health. P2 was also said to be involved in the Bologna massacre of 1980, when a terrorist bomb killed 85 people, but high-ranking figures in Italian intelligence supposedly fabricated evidence to cover Gelli's trail.

P2 are also said to have coordinated the operations of the Mafia and the Vatican Bank, under the aegis of Archbishop Paul Marcinkus, head of the Bank and an alleged P2 member. When John Paul I became pope in 1978 he allegedly threatened to expose P2 and clean house at the Vatican, so, conspiracy theorists claim, P2 had him murdered and then covered up the assassination. P2 is also accused of being behind the murder of Calvi, whose death was apparently rich in Masonic symbolism. Documents hidden in the bottom of a suitcase are said to have revealed that P2 was also formulating a political program known as the *piano di rinascita democratica* – "plan for democratic rebirth" – which involved gaining control of the media to effect a right-wing shift in Italian politics. Conspiracy theorists claim that this plan was more or less implemented by Silvio Berlusconi, a former P2 member, who brought neo-fascist parties into his governing coalition.

The skeptical view

P2 and Gelli probably were involved in some criminal conspiracies, but many of the names on the list found in Gelli's villa proved to have nothing to do with the lodge, skeptics argue. Exhaustive judicial enquiries have failed to find conclusive evidence linking P2 to most of the outrages listed above. Moro was murdered by the Red Brigades, a radical left-wing faction. There is no real evidence that Pope John Paul I planned actions against P2, and he was known to be frail and in poor health and his death was due to natural causes.

Global influence: 35/100

P2 was probably instrumental in setting up and financing shady operations around the world, and almost certainly played a major role in the murky world of 1970s Italian politics and finance.

How to join

Unless you're a Latin American dictator, Mafia banker, or head of the Italian secret services, don't bother applying.

Aum Shinrikyo

Japanese doomsday "Mad
Gassers" cult responsible
for the 1995 Tokyo subway
nerve-gas attack, linked to
energy-weapon conspiracies
and government cover-ups.

Place of origin:	Japan
When:	1980s
Founder(s):	Shoko Ashara
Current status:	Active, Japan

History

Founded by Shoko Asahara in the 1980s, Aum Shinrikyo ("Supreme Truth")
was originally a yoga and health-food sect based loosely on Buddhism. By the
1990s the cult had become apocalyptic in outlook. Recruitment targeted college
graduates and professionals, who were encouraged to hand over most of their
income to the cult and to work in its businesses. Asahara preached a strict
vegetarian diet and claimed to be an Enlightened One and successor to Buddha.

By 1995 the cult was believed to be worth $1.5 billion, with 10,000 adherents
in Japan and 65,000 more around the world, particularly in Russia where Aum
had its secondary focus. The cult also bought property in the Australian outback;
in May 1993 there was an earthquake centered on the location. On March 20,
1995, 12 people were killed and more than 2,000 injured in a Sarin nerve-gas
attack on the Tokyo subway. In the aftermath, chemical and biological weapons
laboratories belonging to the group were uncovered and more than 200 members
of Aum were arrested. Asahara was sentenced to death and currently awaits execution.

The conspiracy theories

Aum Shinrikyo's activities and connections prior to the Tokyo gas attack have led
to numerous conspiracy theories. Asahara believed it was his duty to hasten the
advent of the Apocalypse, to which end he planned to destabilize the Japanese
government with massive terrorist attacks. In Russia, Aum used bribery to gain
access to weapons and training. They attempted numerous attacks with chemical
and biological weapons, including anthrax and botulin releases, and a trial run
for the release of Sarin in 1994. Asahara visited Africa to try to acquire Ebola

virus samples, and visited Belgrade to attempt to steal documents from the Nikola Tesla archives. Tesla was the leading inventor of the electrical age, and in later life boasted of designs for super-weapons such as death rays and earthquake machines. Conspiracy theorists believe that an Aum experiment with Tesla-energy weapons accounts for the earthquake centered on their Australian property.

Despite their prior attacks and many other warnings of their dangerous designs, the authorities somehow failed to act. Conspiracy theorists claim this was because Aum had connections to powerful politicians, such as onetime Governor of Tokyo, Shintaro Ishihara, and to the Yakuza (for whom Aum supposedly made drugs in their labs). It is also suggested that Aum may have been framed for the Sarin attacks by another powerful doomsday cult, Soka Gakkai, which also has links to the Japanese establishment.

The skeptical view

Aum Shinrikyo was a dangerous and delusional cult, but Tesla's energy weapons were always a fantasy, and earthquake generators do not exist. The failure of the authorities to preempt Aum owes more to error than conspiracy.

Global influence: 9/100

Aum Shinrikyo should have alerted the world to what an ambitious terror group can achieve.

How to join

Aleph and Hikari no Wa – splinter groups of Aum – still exist, although prospective members should bear in mind that members have previously been expected to purchase items such as Asahara's urine and semen.

Right Shoko Asahara, the former leader of Aum Shinrikyo, 2006.

Al-Qaeda

Infamous as the organization behind the 9/11 attacks, al-Qaeda is an umbrella organization for extremist Islamist terror groups.

Place of origin:	Afghanistan
When:	1988
Founder(s):	Osama bin Laden
Current status:	Active, worldwide

History

Al-Qaeda means the "base" or "Foundation." It was created in 1988, as the Afghan-Soviet war came to a close. Islamist extremists had flocked to the Afghan cause to help expel the infidel invader, and the experience and confidence gained in this conflict inspired their wider agenda. Al-Qaeda's precursor Makhtab al Khadimat (MAK, Mujahadeen Services Bureau) had been formed in 1984 to provide logistical and training support for the Afghan mujahadeen (holy warriors). A leading light in the MAK was Osama bin Laden, a Saudi millionaire-turned-Islamist extremist. Together with his mentor Abdullah Azzam, bin Laden decided to found a group that would coordinate and facilitate terror attacks in support of their pan-Islamic ideology. In 1988, meetings in Peshawar, Pakistan, led to the announcement of al-Qaeda's existence. When American troops were stationed in Saudi Arabia in the wake of the first Gulf War, al-Qaeda focused on driving them out and striking at American, Israeli, and general Western interests.

Al-Qaeda trained recruits, chose targets, and coordinated policy, but the execution of operations was left to local groups. Around 30 Islamist terror movements across the Islamic world, including the Armed Islamic Group (the GIA, Algeria), Hezbollah (the Party of God, Lebanon), Hamas (Palestine), the Islamic Jihad (Egypt), and Gama'a Islamiyya (Indonesia), are affiliated with al-Qaeda. Some of them were founded or are manned by al-Qaeda trainees.

Major terror attacks linked to al-Qaeda include: the World Trade Center bombing of 1993; the Khobar Tower bombing in Saudi Arabia in 1996; attacks on US embassies in Kenya and Tanzania in 1998; the attack on the USS *Cole* in 2000; the 9/11 attacks of 2001; bombs in Bali, Saudi Arabia, and Morocco in 2002–03; Madrid in March 2004; and London in July 2005. After 9/11,

American-led operations forced al-Qaeda out of its Afghan bases, but it had already redeployed to Pakistan from where it still operates, although its capacity is much reduced and bin Laden himself has been killed.

The conspiracy theories

The 9/11 attacks have become the most intense focus of conspiracy theories since the Kennedy assassination, and many of these theories revolve around al-Qaeda's backers and its connections with the security apparatus of various states, including the USA. The theories run the gamut from well-informed and plausible to baroque Plot Theory fantasies.

According to assorted paranoiacs, al-Qaeda is believed to have been the creation of the CIA, to be protected by the intelligence services of Pakistan, Iran, and the Gulf States, and to be funded by Gulf princes directing their billions to wage a secret war against the West. The CIA are said to have known that the 9/11 hijackers were in America, either because they thought they were double-agents or because they had created al-Qaeda to provoke anti-Islamic sentiment and provide a pretext for America's response (for example, the invasion of Iraq, massive military spending, restrictions on civil liberties). Similarly, Israel's Mossad and the wider Illuminati conspiracy are both accused of being the true powers behind al-Qaeda.

The skeptical view

The extreme anti-American agenda and ideology of al-Qaeda have repeatedly been made very clear, so claims of American involvement are ridiculous, say the skeptics. American failure to prevent 9/11 was due to intelligence failures, not conspiracy.

Global influence: 42/100

Although al-Qaeda is now much diminished, the 9/11 attacks achieved their aim: provoking a massive and polarizing response from the West and its allies.

How to join

Attempting to join a deranged apocalyptic terror sect seems ill-advised, especially since you may find yourself in Guantanamo Bay.

Part Five:
Criminal Societies

Thuggee

Indian sect who murdered travelers as a sacrament to the goddess Kali, until they were stamped out by the British colonial authorities in the 19th century.

Place of origin:	Northern India
When:	ca. 17th–19th century
Founder(s):	Unknown
Current status:	Defunct

History

Thug or Thuggee means "deceiver," though in southern India they were known as Phansigari, "stranglers." An article by Richard Sherwood on the Phansigari appeared in the *Madras Literary Gazette* in 1816 setting out their customs and beliefs. A hereditary society of killers worshipping the goddess Kali, they practiced ritual murder as a form of devotion. Their method of killing was strangulation, reflecting the myth of Kali's battle with a demon whose blood created copies of himself if it touched the ground. Kali created the first Thuggee to destroy the cloned demons.

Victims were murdered with the Rumal, a cloth noose worn about the waist. There were strict rules on permissible victims, and to maintain secrecy no witnesses could be left alive. It was claimed that the Thuggee had prehistoric roots, but most experts believe they probably arose in medieval times. The death toll attributed to their actions ranges from millions to 50,000, which even at the lower figure makes them one of the deadliest secret societies.

A young British officer named William Sleeman devoted himself to the capture of the Thuggee. Eventually there was an entire intelligence service, the Thuggee Daftar (Thug Office), and more than 3,000 Thugs were apprehended between 1831 and 1837. The sect finally died out sometime in the late 19th century.

The conspiracy theories

The Thuggee fulfilled contemporary prejudices about the dark and degenerate East, and their bizarre cult of death was conflated with equally disturbing Tantric sexual practices. It was said that the female counterparts of the male

Thugs indulged in insatiable sexual perversion as a form of Kali worship, while Thuggee strangling was given homoerotic overtones. The colonial authorities tended also to conflate organized criminal acts like those committed by the Thuggee with political challenge to their rule, and the Thuggee were painted as anticolonial agitators, while their successful suppression was adduced as evidence that the Indians not only benefited from but needed benevolent colonial rule. For Ariosophist/Theosophist conspiracy theorists, the Thuggee were evidence of the true nature of non-Aryan root races, archaic foot soldiers in the cosmic battle between Aryans and their degenerate enemies.

The skeptical view

The extent and antiquity of the Thuggee were probably exaggerated and the lurid sexual elements of their legend invented.

Global influence: 7/100

Between 1600 and 1830 the Thuggee presented a genuine threat to travelers, but today they are best known as the villains from *Indiana Jones and the Temple of Doom*.

How to join

Membership was hereditary, except occasionally in the case of young boys caught up in an attack, who might be initiated into the cult of Thuggee.

Above A group of Thugs, ca. 1865, Peshawar.

Triads

Chinese criminal fraternities with mystical and occult elements and a history of political involvement, which spread around the world with the Chinese diaspora.

Place of origin:	China
When:	Qing dynasty (1644–1912)
Founder(s):	Unknown
Current status:	Active, worldwide

History

The Triads are Chinese criminal secret societies; the term derives from the original titles of some of the societies, or *hui*, which involved the three aspects of the cosmos: man, heaven, and earth. Early *hui* are said to have included the Heaven and Earth Society (Tiandihui), the Three Dots Society (Sandianhui), the Three Unities Society (Sanhehui), and the Hong League (Hung Mun). The origins of the Triads are contentious (see below), but they are probably related to other Chinese sects and societies that mixed martial arts with occult practices and religious beliefs (see Boxers, page 103).

Triad *hui* are characterized by oaths of brotherhood (*guanxi*), with younger "brothers" expected to obey the Chinese tradition of rigid obedience to older ones. At the head of each *hui* is a chief, with two lieutenants filling the traditional offices of Incense Master (the religious overseer) and the Vanguard (in charge of administration and arms). Five lower-ranked officers each oversee a specific area of responsibility, including a welfare section that traditionally took care of funerals. For the Chinese overseas, this function was especially important because it was a requirement to be buried in China. The overseas Triads, known as Tongs, gained influence from their role in this regard.

In late imperial China, the Triads controlled gambling but also got involved in politics, supporting uprisings such as the Boxer rebellion (see page 103) and Sun Yat Sen's successful republican campaign to end imperial rule. After the Second World War, the Triads threw their lot in with the Nationalists and were subsequently suppressed by the communists, surviving in Hong Kong, Taiwan, and overseas. From their power base in Hong Kong, where there were an estimated 300,000 members in 1947, the Triads took control of the drug traffic out of Southeast Asia, also diversifying into people smuggling and trading in endangered species.

The conspiracy theories

According to the Triads' own legends, they sprang up as a nativist movement to oppose the conquest of China by the foreign Manchu, or Qing, dynasty. Governed by the maxim "defeat the Qing, restore the Ming" (the previous, native dynasty), they championed the cause of the weak and defenseless against the cruel Manchu overlords. Esoteric initiation practices, such as the "hanging the lantern" ritual, in which initiates are bound together for a symbolic journey to a new identity as *hui* members, were believed to help give the Triads magical powers such as invulnerability.

The skeptical view

The true origins of the Triads are more recent than their legends suggest, and can be traced back to the foundation of the Heaven and Earth Society at the Guanyinting (Goddess of Mercy pavilion) in Gaoxi township, Fujian province, in the southeast of China, in 1761 or 1762. Originally they were a mutual aid fraternity, similar to the Oddfellows (a mutual aid fraternity in Britain and America in the 18th and 19th centuries). Impoverished and marginalized, they were easily drawn into crime. Today their mystical and occult window-dressing conceals straightforward criminality.

Global influence: 10/100

The Triads and the Tong have been a major influence in Chinese communities around the world.

How to join

Learn to speak Chinese and brush up on your martial arts and invulnerability magic.

Yakuza

Japanese crime clans or families; the largest organized crime organization in the world they occupy an oddly traditional role in Japanese society.

Place of origin:	Japan
When:	17th century
Founder(s):	Unknown
Current status:	Active, Japan

History

Yakuza means "good for nothing" or "worthless" – it comes from the Japanese for "8, 9, 3," referring to a busted hand in a traditional blackjack-like card game. Worn as a badge of pride, the name signifies something about the nonconformist attitude of the Yakuza in opposition to traditional Japanese society. They are the postwar incarnation of Japanese criminal societies with roots in the late medieval era, supposedly dating back to 16th-century gangs of lordless samurai, or ronin, who turned to banditry.

Modern Yakuza still adopt some samurai stylings, considering themselves a cut above petty criminals. A Kobun (apprentice or "child") swears absolute loyalty to a boss or *oyabun* ("father"), who in turn swears to protect him. Members are heavily tattooed across the entire body to demonstrate their commitment. A Yakuza who transgresses or offends his *obayun* is expected to practice *yubizume* – cutting off the last joint of the little finger on his left hand, a reference to a traditional gambling penalty. Prewar Yakuza concentrated on gambling and extortion, but in the postwar era, when their numbers exploded, reaching a high of around 185,000 in 1963, the Yakuza diversified into a dizzying range of activities, both illegal and legitimate. Today their numbers have declined but there are still around 80,000 Yakuza and associates in hundreds of gangs.

The conspiracy theories

The Yakuza claim to have originated as Robin Hood-style bandits, known as *machi-yokko* (servants of the town, or common people). One of the most remarkable features of the Yakuza is their brazen visibility; their businesses and hang-outs are often clearly signposted, and the big Yakuza conglomerates have corporate-style head offices. Conspiracy theorists link this to their close connections with the Japanese political and military establishment, with its roots in shared ultra-nationalist ideology. These links were forged in the early 20th century when the ultra-nationalist secret intelligence service, Black Dragon, was covertly advancing Japan's imperialist ambitions, with the help of Yakuza funding. Today these murky links endure – for instance, the Yakuza were implicated in the scandal surrounding official failure to shut down Aum Shinrikyo before it launched its Tokyo subway nerve-gas attacks (see page 116). Some claim that racist and ultra-nationalist elements within the military and the establishment continue to protect the Yakuza.

The skeptical view

Yakuza claims about their "good guy" origins are suspiciously similar to those of the Triads (see page 124) and the Mafia (see page 135); in reality, they were relatively small fry until after the Second World War. Japanese society was shattered by the war, leaving a power vacuum the Yakuza were quick to fill (hence their runaway expansion in the 1950s), while the occupying Americans preferred to turn a blind eye to such an entrenched social phenomenon. Ironically, the Yakuza made their early fortunes by smuggling guns, banned by the occupying authorities. For all their samurai posturing, the true models of the Yakuza have long been American gangsters, and many still favor Rat Pack-era suits and pompadours. Though tolerated because they maintain relative order in the criminal underworld, a continued official crackdown means they are in irreversible decline.

Global influence: 15/100

Not only a major influence on contemporary global crime, the Yakuza may also have been a hidden hand behind Japan's early 20th-century imperial expansion.

How to join

Modern Yakuza are often drawn from the *bosozuku* (speed tribes), motorcycle-fetishizing street punks – so buy a bike and get a lot of tattoos.

Cosa Nostra

The Sicilian mafia, the template for organized crime associations around the world, have all the characteristics of a secret society, from initiation to shadowy agenda.

Place of origin:	Sicily
When:	mid 19th century
Founder(s):	Unknown
Current status:	Active, Sicily

History

The Cosa Nostra ("Our Affair"), is one of the names given to the Sicilian mafia, or organized crime associations. In practice the Cosa Nostra is composed of different "families" (societies or clans based on geography and loose kinship ties), which compete but nonetheless observe universal rules and customs.

The Cosa Nostra is a secret society in which each family is roughly equivalent to a lodge. Like other secret societies, the Cosa Nostra keeps its membership secret and tries to conceal its agenda, structure, and rituals. Nonetheless, it is known that each family is led by a *capo* or *capofamiglia*, who has a *consigliere* (counselor) to advise him, and delegates authority to captains who each run their own crew. Below the captains are soldiers who are directly responsible for earning money, tithes on which are fed back up the chain. New members undergo an initiation ritual, in which blood is dripped onto a picture of a saint, which is then burned to ashes, symbolizing the irreversible nature of the *mafiosi* commitment. Oaths are sworn, and new *mafiosi* are expected to abide by a strict code on pain of death. The most important of these codes is *omertà*, the code of silence, which prevents Cosa Nostra members and everyone in their community from divulging information on mafia activities.

The conspiracy theories

The close relationship between the Cosa Nostra and politicians in Sicily and Italy in general has led to a host of conspiracy theories, many of them taken seriously enough to result in trials and convictions. Via the machinations of P2 and Lico Gelli (see page 113), for instance, the Cosa Nostra were supposedly involved in financing and arming Gladio-style operations (see page 111), the strategy of tension (see page 112), and financial crimes on an epic scale relating to the Vatican Bank and some of Italy's leading private banks (see page 113). One accusation is that P2 brokered a money-laundering deal where the Vatican Bank swapped hundreds of millions of dollars worth of shares for dirty drug money from the Cosa Nostra. The Cosa Nostra were particularly associated with Italian Prime Minister Giulio Andreotti, until he turned on them once in office and they murdered his Sicilian lieutenant Salvo Lima, in 1992.

The skeptical view

Colorful legends of perpetuation notwithstanding, the origin of the Cosa Nostra can probably be traced back to the violent and difficult history of Sicily. Ruled

Above Giovanni Nicchi, considered to be one of the leading mafiosi of Cosa Nostra, arrives in the police headquarters after being arrested on December 5, 2009, in Palermo, Italy.

and exploited by a series of foreign powers, the indigenous inhabitants developed a tradition of self-reliance and self-defense, separated from the alien ruling cultures by a firewall of honor and silence codes.

In the 19th century these village militia/gangs had become established as the Tenebrosi Sodalizi, the Dark Brotherhoods, each based around a small town or area. Much of Sicily was carved up into large estates belonging to absentee landlords, who let the Brotherhoods run things in return for order and stability. When Unification came, and the political dispensation of Italy changed, the Brotherhoods were already embedded in society. New political parties struck a pact with them; in return for votes, the authorities would tolerate the criminal associations. By the turn of the century, the Sicilian mafia was calling itself the Cosa Nostra or La Società Onorata, the Honored Society, and constituted almost a shadow state. The Fascists under Mussolini checked their influence and locked up many of the *mafiosi* in 1922, but when the Allies invaded they viewed the Cosa Nostra as useful local allies, freeing the hoodlums who went on to flourish in the post-war era, renewing their long-running pact with the political system, specifically with the now-defunct Christian Democratic Party. Thanks to media sensationalism, however, the extent of these mafia-government conspiracies has been overstated, and there is no evidence of any links between the Cosa Nostra and fantastical Gladio conspiracies.

Global influence: 35/100

On top of their influence on Italian politics, the Cosa Nostra are major players in international drugs-, people-, and arms-trafficking, and the model and prototype of organized crime associations all over the world.

How to join

You need to be associated by blood or geographical ties with the home base of a Cosa Nostra family before you can be considered for membership.

Camorra

Organized crime fraternity of Naples, the Camorra are the most numerous Italian mafia, their criminal conspiracies firmly embedded in the fabric of their city, socially and, possibly, physically.

Place of origin:	Italy
When:	ca. 18th century
Founder(s):	Unknown
Current status:	Active, Italy

History

Official records of Camorra meetings and constitutions show that as early as 1820 they had a distinct structure, although they are considered much less hierarchical than the Sicilian Cosa Nostra, with a more horizontal structure of different and competing family-based clans, grouped in a loose confederation.

The Bourbon rulers of Naples (then an independent state) may have used the Camorra as a paramilitary force to control their unruly kingdom, but this deal backfired when the Camorristi helped depose the monarchy in 1861, aligning themselves with Garibaldi's unification movement. The group reached the zenith of their power in the 1880s, but the authorities hit back in a campaign culminating in a 1911 trial that temporarily broke the power of the Camorra. After the Second World War they reestablished themselves through control of cigarette smuggling, later linking up with the Sicilian mafia to use their smuggling networks to move heroin. More recently, so many male members have been arrested that wives and sisters have increasingly taken over criminal operations.

The Camorra is known for its brutal initiation rituals, which involve knife-wielding feats of machismo. According to one account, initiates were pitted against each other in a knife-fight and expected to grab their opponent's blade; in another, the initiate attempted to snatch a coin from the floor while Camorristi slashed at his hand. A heavily scarred hand is thus a telltale sign of initiation.

The conspiracy theories

Legend has it that the Camorra are descended from a Spanish criminal secret society, the Garduna, dating back to 1417, which transferred to Naples when it became a Spanish possession. In one version, a Spanish knight named Raimondo Gamur set up the Neapolitan gang, which was named for him; in another version three Spanish brothers founded the mafia in Sicily, Naples, and Calabria. Originally the Camorra were called the Bella Società Riformata, and were modeled on the Carbonari (see page 96), with two grades – the Società Minore and the Società Maggiore.

The Camorra are so embedded in the lower echelons of Neapolitan society that their criminal way of life is simply known as the System. Using their financial and social muscle to influence politics, they are suspected of involvement in all public works. In the aftermath of the 1980 Campania earthquake the Camorra grew fat off massive reconstruction contracts, combining their control of construction and waste-disposal to rebuild parts of Naples with concrete laced with toxic waste.

The skeptical view

Even the Legends of Perpetuation recognize that the Camorra originated as a prison gang, but they have no validity beyond this. They probably date to the early 19th century, a period of chaos and breakdown of central authority attending the Napoleonic invasion of Naples and the subsequent restoration of the Bourbon monarchy.

Global influence: 20/100

A key link in the international heroin trade, the Camorra is also believed to control a significant chunk of the Neapolitan economy.

How to join

As with other mafia groups, membership depends on family and place of origin.

'Ndrangheta

Thought to be the richest and most powerful Italian organized crime society, the origins and structure of the 'Ndrangheta are shrouded in mystery.

Place of origin:	Italy
When:	ca.1860s
Founder(s):	Unknown
Current status:	Active, Italy

History

The 'Ndrangheta is the organized criminal fraternity in Calabria, at the extreme southern tip of Italy. Its origins are unclear although it is believed to have started as a prison gang in similar fashion to the Camorra, or, according to the FBI, it may have been founded by exiled Sicilians. Given that Calabria was a stronghold of 19th-century republicanism, it seems highly plausible that early forms of the 'Ndrangheta were inspired by the Carbonari (see page 96).

Calabria has long been one of Italy's poorest and politically isolated regions, and the 'Ndrangheta operated in relative freedom for a century, until, in the 1970s, it started kidnapping wealthy individuals from the north and bringing them back to the rugged mountainous interior region of Aspromonte. With funds rolling in from ransoms, the 'Ndrangheta then expanded into drug smuggling.

Despite subsequent bloody internal feuding, the 'Ndrangheta has proven extremely resistant to police action, allowing it to become the richest and most powerful Italian mafia, with 7,000 members versus the Cosa Nostra's 5,000. It is believed to be based strongly on direct blood ties, which increases the adherence of members to values of *omertà*, making turncoats and informers much less common. Also, they are thought to have a less hierarchical, pyramidal-structure than the Cosa Nostra, making their organization harder to disrupt.

The conspiracy theories

In 2005 Francesco Fortugno, deputy speaker of the Calabrian regional parliament, was shot dead in a suspected 'Ndrangheta assassination. Conspiracy theories link his murder to the politics surrounding plans to build a huge suspension bridge over the Straits of Messina separating Calabria from Sicily. Supposedly the 'Ndrangheta delivered many votes to Fortugno's party on the premise that they would back the bridge project, from which the Calabrian mafia intended to profit handsomely. When the government rejected the project, it is said the 'Ndrangheta had Fortugno murdered as a message to reconsider.

The 'Ndrangheta are believed to be the Italian mafia with the widest global contacts, and are particularly linked to the South American drug trade. The latest conspiracy theory to surface links them directly to Mexico's powerful Zeta cartel; they are said to be behind billions of dollars of cocaine imports to Europe.

The skeptical view

The Berlusconi government insisted that the Messina Straits Bridge project is legitimate and a much-needed infrastructure boost to a poor region, while the authorities claim that a series of surveillance operations culminating in a wave of arrests in early 2011 has disrupted 'Ndrangheta operations.

Global influence: 30/100

Quite apart from their key role in the global drug trade, the 'Ndrangheta dominate their domestic economy. The Italian authorities estimate their annual

turnover at over 35 billion euros, making them bigger than Fiat and larger than Calabria's entire legal economy – equivalent to 3 percent of Italy's gross domestic product.

How to join

You need to be born to an 'Ndrangheta family to become a *Giovane d'onore* (young man of honor).

Left The suspected head of 'Ndrangheta, Salvatore Coluccio, is escorted by police special forces following his arrest on May 10, 2009.

American Mafia

Thanks to movies, books, and TV shows, the American Mafia is the best-known criminal fraternity in the world; but is there really any such thing as the Mafia?

Place of origin:	USA
When:	Late 1800s
Founder(s):	Unknown
Current status:	Uncertain, USA

History

In 1951, Senator Estes Kefauver began a series of Congressional hearings into the activities of organized crime associations in the United States. The sensational testimony of *mafiosi* informants seemed to reveal the existence of a huge criminal conspiracy run by Italian-American mob families, which controlled crime in America from illegal gambling to labor racketeering. The explosive growth of the drugs trade led to enormous profits for the Mafia in the 1960s and '70s, but crackdowns by the authorities in the '80s and '90s led to the decline of the Mafia and their usurpation by criminal associations of other ethnicities and nationalities.

The American Mafia is run on similar lines to its Sicilian version (see page 128), with "families" equivalent to lodges, each with a *capo* and lesser ranks. Initiation ceremonies seem to be similar, and in theory American *mafiosi* are expected to observe similar rules and codes of honor.

The conspiracy theories

According to some experts, the conventional account of the development and history of the American Mafia is itself a conspiracy theory. The usual version is that émigrés from Sicily and other poor parts of Italy where mafia presence was strong brought their criminal fraternities with them from the old country. In early 20th-century America these fraternities operated as La Mano Nera, the Black Hand, using threatening notes to extort money from Italian-American businessmen, signing them with the imprint of a black hand. Prohibition created a huge and lucrative market for bootlegging, which led to an explosive growth in the Mafia, but also triggered a series of destructive turf wars. Determined to modernize the Mafia, a new guard led by Al Capone and Lucky Luciano swept away the old Sicilian "Mustache Petes" and set up the Commission, which regulated Mafia activities.

In the postwar period, the Mafia developed Las Vegas and invested millions in Cuba, which they lost when Fidel Castro led a revolution there. Determined to get their revenge, the Mafia worked with the CIA to set up the Bay of Pigs invasion, the ill-fated attempt to launch a counter-coup in Cuba in 1961. Convinced that John F. Kennedy (whom they had helped elect) had betrayed them, some conspiracy theorists believe they then helped to assassinate him. Meanwhile, the FBI under J. Edgar Hoover insisted there was no such thing as the Mafia, supposedly because the Mob was blackmailing him with photos revealing his homosexuality.

The skeptical view

Hoover was right, skeptics claim. The Mafia as a national conspiracy was invented to give politicians an easy target for law-and-order rhetoric and law enforcement agencies a way to secure funding. The Black Hand phenomenon, for instance, was created by disparate criminals and gangs, most of them not Italian. Similarly, Italian-American mobsters were neither the only nor even the dominant force during Prohibition; organized crime has always been the preserve of independent gangsters and small gangs of varying ethnicities, with no central coordination or control. Fictional depictions of the American Mafia have fed back into the mythical version peddled by the authorities, say the skeptics.

Global influence: 30/100

Even if the American Mafia is partly a construct, mafia-like organized crime has played a major role in America's society, economy, and politics, at the same time creating cultural templates of enduring influence.

How to join

If there's no such thing as the Mafia, it must be impossible to join.

Murder Inc.

A murderous secret society within a secret society, Murder Inc. was the ruthless enforcement arm of America's "National Crime Syndicate" in the 1930s and '40s.

Place of origin:	USA
When:	1920s–1940s
Founder(s):	Unknown
Current status:	Defunct

History

According to the conventional history of the American Mafia (see page 135), the disparate mobs of Prohibition-era America were forged into something much grander by gangster Charles "Lucky" Luciano (nicknamed for having survived a brutal gangland attack) in the 1930s. By the time Prohibition was repealed, there were organized crime outfits in every major city of America, with the greatest concentration in New York. Although there were major gang leaders, and even a de facto *capo di tutto capi* ("boss of all the bosses") in the person of Giuseppe "Joe the Boss" Masseria, the Mafia were not fit for purpose. At least this was the sentiment of Lucky Luciano, one of Masseria's lieutenants at the time, who believed his boss's old school refusal to deal with non-Sicilians, and even to hold grudges against Sicilians from the "wrong village," would hold back organized crime. Luciano had Masseria killed and took over his operations. When mobster Johnny Torrio touted the idea of an overarching Syndicate to coordinate and control criminal associations across the country, Luciano and his colleague Lepke Buchalter were enthusiastic. A key element of their plan was that a board of directors would keep the various mobs in line, and they needed muscle to enforce their edicts. This is where Murder Inc. was born.

The conspiracy theories

According to the version of the Murder Inc. story authored by Burton Turkus, a district attorney who played a major role in prosecuting the alleged killer crew, Murder Inc. comprised a small group of mobsters from Brownsville in Brooklyn. Buchalter relied on them to do his dirty work and they were renowned for their professionalism and precision. Under Buchalter's aegis, they became the deadliest outfit in America. Calling themselves the Troop, they committed more than a hundred murders at the behest of the Syndicate, evading justice thanks to the political and judicial connections of Buchalter and others.

A sustained assault on their organization by crusading District Attorney Thomas Dewey caused Murder Inc. to go on a killing spree, attempting to rub out any one who might give them away. This had the effect of frightening potential victims into cooperating with the authorities, and during 1940 and 1941, Dewey landed a series of increasingly big fish, culminating in Abe "Kid Twist" Reles, a key member of Murder Inc. Reles spilled the beans on the entire operation, but Buchalter used his political contacts to delay his own conviction, during which time Reles mysteriously "fell" from a high window despite being under armed guard. Eventually Buchalter was sent to the chair in 1944 and the members of Murder Inc. were all either locked up or dead. As a final gambit to save his life, Buchalter is said to have offered Dewey (by now the governor of New York and running for president) explosive information on major political figures in bed with the Mob, information that could win him the election. Dewey turned him down.

The skeptical view

The tale of Murder Inc. is too far-fetched to be true for some. To what extent they or the Syndicate actually existed outside of the imaginations of the likes of Turkus is unclear. Dewey turned down Buchalter's mysterious offer because the mobster had no such secret information, while Reles died trying to escape.

Global influence: 9/100

Murder Inc. was a short-lived episode in the history of American organized crime that has probably been over-hyped and mythologized.

How to join

Only stone-cold killers need apply.

Glossary

adept: someone who has mastered magic and occult practices.

alchemy: mystical chemistry concerned with material and spiritual transformation and the recovery of ancient wisdom.

anticommunism: an ideology concerned with combating Communism in any form by any means necessary.

Ariosophy: occult, anti-Semitic belief system based on Germanic mysticism, pseudoscience, and pseudohistory.

bioterror: terrorism carried out with biological weapons, such as anthrax.

black helicopters: in conspiracy circles, unmarked helicopters used by secret agencies for covert ops.

black ops: illegal covert operations.

brainwashed: caused to believe or act in some fashion contrary to normal, through hypnosis or some other form of mind control.

CIA: Central Intelligence Agency; the foreign intelligence agency of the United States, set up in 1945 as the successor to the Office of Strategic Services.

conspiracy: a secret plan by two or more people to do something illegal or immoral.

Council on Foreign Relations: private U.S. think-tank/discussion group concerned with improving U.S. foreign policy and relations and developing foreign policy talent.

cover-up: an attempt to prevent people from finding out about something, particularly something that should not have happened in the first place.

covert ops: operations or actions carried out in secret or undercover.

Craft, the: another term for Freemasonry.

Degree: rank, achievement, or level within a Masonic or other occult society.

disinformation: information intended to mislead.

deism: the belief that all religions encode underlying truths amenable to rational enquiry.

esoteric: secret, intelligible only to the initiated or those with special knowledge.

false memory: bogus memories created by hypnosis or other forms of therapy, which are believed by the individual concerned to be genuine.

gnosticism: religious tradition that stresses individual contact with the divine, based on belief that the material world is corrupt but every soul contains a spark of divine essence.

Hermes Trismegistus: mythical founder of the Hermetic mysteries, concerned with alchemy and other lost ancient wisdom.

Hermetic: relating to alchemy and other occult traditions.

Hyperborea: mythical lost lands in the far north, claimed as homeland of Aryan peoples (see also Thule).

Kabbalah (also Cabala and Qabala): ancient Jewish tradition of mystic interpretation of holy works using esoteric practices.

Legends of Perpetuation: spurious accounts of the great antiquity of certain Masonic rites, degrees, and societies.

Magus/magi: priestly caste of ancient Persia; later a term for magicians or occult adepts.

Manchurian candidate: a brainwashed assassin activated by posthypnotic suggestion; from the book and movie *The Manchurian Candidate.*

militia: a military force raised from the civilian population; in U.S. context, often refers to armed right-wing survivalists and/or antigovernmental groups.

mind control: causing someone to think or behave in some way without their conscious assent or awareness.

money laundering: handling illegally obtained ("dirty") money so that it appears to have a legitimate source.

Mysteries: secret ancient religions or religious rites practiced only by the initiated.

Neo-Rosicrucian: concerned with Rosicrucian themes but having no historical links to the original Rosicrucians, despite bogus claims to contrary.

New World Order (NWO): supposed one-world government by corrupt elites that already exists in secret and, in the guise of various secret societies, is plotting for the day when it can reveal itself and openly implement its tyrannical program.

occult: hidden; refers to mystical, magical, or esoteric learning only available to the initiated.

parapolitics: politics carried out through underhand means (e.g. assassination, smear campaigns, etc.).

pseudoscience: a system of thought and practice that makes bogus claims to be scientific and uses the trappings of science, such as scientific jargon, to lend authority to itself.

reverse engineering: the process of working backward from super-advanced alien technology to arrive at technology that humans can understand and use.

Root races: racist pseudoscientific theory advanced by the Theosophical Society to explain human origins.

saucer retrieval: recovery of crashed alien spacecraft for study and concealment.

Theosophy: belief that study of religion can reveal fundamental truths common to all.

Thule: mythical northern homeland of the Aryan peoples.

Trilateral Commission: private think-tank/discussion group founded in 1973 to promote cooperation between Japan, North America, and Europe.

UFO: Unidentified Flying Object; technically any unexplained aerial phenomenon, but usually used to mean an alien spacecraft.

ufology: the study of UFOs and related issues; carried out by ufologists.

Sources

Books

Bennet, Richard M. *Conspiracies: Plots, Lies and Cover-Ups*. Virgin, 2003

Coward, Barry, Ed. *Conspiracies and Conspiracy Theory in Early Modern Europe: From the Waldensians to the French Revolution*. Ashgate, 2004

Goodrick-Clarke, Nicholas. *Occult Roots of Nazism: Secret Aryan Cults and Their Influence on Nazi Ideology*. NYU Press, 1993

Howe, Ellic. *The Magicians of the Golden Dawn: A Documentary History of a Magical Order, 1887-1923*. Taylor & Francis, 1972

Hutchison, Robert. *Their Kingdom Come: Inside the Secret World of Opus Dei*. Corgi, 2005

Mackey, Albert Gallatin, and H. L. Haywood. *Encyclopedia of Freemasonry*. Kessinger Publishing, 2003

Knight, Peter. *Conspiracy Theories in American History: An Encyclopaedia*. ABC-CLIO, 2003

Websites

www.americanmafia.com
www.newadvent.org/cathen
www.freemasonry.bcy.ca
www.sacred-texts.com
www.lobster-magazine.co.uk

www.counterpunch.org
www.parascope.com
www.konformist.com
www.paranoiamagazine.com

Index

Picture credits:
Alamy: pp. 34, 39, 49, 67, 76, 80, 87, 97; Corbis: pp. 19, 22, 27, 52, 61, 72, 104, 117;
Getty: 11, 107, 109, 123, 129, 134; Topfoto: pp. 32, 44, 57, 92, 114.